Java® Performance Companion

Java® Performance Companion

Charlie Hunt
Monica Beckwith
Poonam Parhar
Bengt Rutisson

✝✝Addison-Wesley

Boston • Columbus • Indianapolis • New York • San Francisco • Amsterdam • Cape Town
Dubai • London • Madrid • Milan • Munich • Paris • Montreal • Toronto • Delhi • Mexico City
São Paulo • Sidney • Hong Kong • Seoul • Singapore • Taipei • Tokyo

For information about buying this title in bulk quantities, or for special sales opportunities (which may include electronic versions; custom cover designs; and content particular to your business, training goals, marketing focus, or branding interests), please contact our corporate sales department at corpsales@pearsoned.com or (800) 382-3419.

For government sales inquiries, please contact governmentsales@pearsoned.com.

For questions about sales outside the United States, please contact intlcs@pearson.com.

Visit us on the Web: informit.com/aw

Cataloging-in-Publication Data is on file with the Library of Congress.

Copyright © 2016 Pearson Education, Inc.

ISBN-13: 978-0-13-379682-7
ISBN-10: 0-13-379682-5

Text printed in the United States on recycled paper at RR Donnelley in Crawfordsville, Indiana.
1 16

Contents

Preface

Welcome to the *Java® Performance Companion*. This book offers companion material to *Java™ Performance* [1], which was first published in September 2011. Although the additional topics covered in this book are not as broad as the material in *Java™ Performance*, they go into enormous detail. The topics covered in this book are the G1 garbage collector, also known as the Garbage First garbage collector, and the Java HotSpot VM Serviceability Agent. There is also an appendix that covers additional HotSpot VM command-line options of interest that were not included in the *Java™ Performance* appendix on HotSpot VM command-line options.

If you are currently using Java 8, have interest in migrating to Java 8, or have plans for using Java 9, you will likely be either evaluating G1 GC or already using it. Hence, the information in this book will be useful to you. If you have interest in diagnosing unexpected HotSpot VM failures, or in learning more about the details of a modern Java Virtual Machine, this book's content on the HotSpot VM Serviceability Agent should be of value to you, too. The HotSpot VM Serviceability Agent is the tool of choice for not only HotSpot VM developers but also the Oracle support engineers whose daily job involves diagnosing and troubleshooting unexpected HotSpot VM behavior.

This book begins with an overview of the G1 garbage collector by offering some context around why G1 was implemented and included in HotSpot VM as a GC. It then goes on to offer an overview of how the G1 garbage collector works. This chapter is followed by two additional chapters on G1. The first is an in-depth description of the internals of G1. If you already have a good understanding of how the G1 garbage collector works, and either have a need to further fine-tune G1 or want to know more about its inner workings, this chapter would be a great place to start. The third chapter on G1 is all about fine-tuning G1 for your application. One of the main design points for G1 was to simplify the tuning required to realize good performance. For instance, the major inputs into G1 are the initial and maximum Java heap size it can use, and a maximum GC pause time you are willing to tolerate. From there G1 will attempt to adaptively adjust to meet those inputs while it executes your application. In circumstances where you would like to achieve better performance, or you would like to do some additional tuning on G1, this chapter has the information you are looking for.

The remaining chapter is dedicated entirely to the HotSpot VM Serviceability Agent. This chapter provides an in-depth description of and instructions for how to use the Serviceability Agent. If you have interest in learning more about the internals of the HotSpot VM, or how to troubleshoot and diagnose unexpected HotSpot VM issues, this is a good chapter for you. In this chapter you will learn how to use the HotSpot VM Serviceability Agent to observe and analyze HotSpot VM behavior in a variety of ways through examples and illustrations.

Last, there is an appendix that includes HotSpot VM command-line options that were not included in *Java™ Performance*'s appendix on HotSpot VM command-line options. Many of the HotSpot VM command-line options found in the appendix are related to G1. And, rather than merely listing these options with only a description, an attempt is made to also mention when it is appropriate to use them.

References

[1] Charlie Hunt and Binu John. *Java™ Performance*. Addison-Wesley, Upper Saddle River, NJ, 2012. ISBN 978-0-13-714252-1.

Register your copy of *Java® Performance Companion* at informit.com for convenient access to downloads, updates, and corrections as they become available. To start the registration process, go to informit.com/register and log in or create an account. Enter the product ISBN (9780133796827) and click Submit. Once the process is complete, you will find any available bonus content under "Registered Products."

Acknowledgments

Charlie Hunt

For those who have ever considered writing a book, or are curious about the effort involved in doing so, the book-writing experience is a major undertaking! For me it just would not have happened without the help of so many people. I cannot begin to mention everyone who made this possible.

In an attempt to at least name those who have had a profound impact on this book getting drafted and eventually into print, I would first like to thank my coauthors, Monica Beckwith, Bengt Rutisson, and Poonam Parhar. When the idea of doing a companion book to *Java™ Performance* first surfaced, I thought it would be great to offer the opportunity to these talented HotSpot VM engineers to showcase their expertise. I am sure I have learned much more from each of them than they have learned from me. I could not be prouder of their contributions to this book.

I also extend sincere thanks to Monica Beckwith for her persistence and passion in sharing her in-depth knowledge of G1 GC. In the early days of G1, I had the pleasure of working with Monica on a daily basis on G1 performance, eventually handing off full reins to her. She has done an exceptional job with driving G1's performance and sharing her G1 knowledge.

I also have to explicitly call out Poonam Parhar and thank her for her patience. Poonam so patiently waited for the other contributors to complete their initial drafts—patiently as in years of patience! Had all of us finished our drafts in a timely way, this book probably would have been on the shelf at least two years earlier.

I also extend my thanks to the entire HotSpot VM team, the HotSpot GC engineering team, and in particular the G1 GC engineers, both past and present.

And to the reviewers of the material in this book: Paul Hohensee for his relentless attention to detail and incredible suggestions for improved readability, and Tony Printezis for his thorough review of the gory details of G1 GC and recommended tuning of G1.

Thanks also to John Cuthbertson for sharing his knowledge of G1. John also happens to be one of the most talented concurrency troubleshooting engineers I have ever worked with. I don't think I ever saw a situation where I was able to stump him with some bizarre observation about G1 that was clearly some kind of concurrency bug. He was always able to track it down.

And to Bernard Traversat and Georges Saab for their support and encouragement in pulling together material for a follow-on to *Java™ Performance*.

And obviously thanks to Greg Doench, our editor, for his patience with our many delays in delivering drafts, completing reviews, and getting the manuscript in shape to put in his hands.

Last, thanks to my wife, Barb, and son, Boyd, for putting up with yet another round of the book-writing experience!

Monica Beckwith

I felt honored when I was approached by my mentor Charlie Hunt to write a few chapters for this book. I didn't have the slightest idea that it would take me so long. So, my first set of thanks goes to my fellow writers for their patience and to Charlie for his persistence and encouragement throughout. While we are talking about encouragement, I want to thank my hubby, Ben Beckwith—when he saw my frustration he had nothing but words of encouragement for me. He was also the initial reviewer of my drafts. Thank you, Ben. And then, of course, my two kiddos, Annika and Bodin, and my mom, Usha, who have been nothing but supportive of me and of this book.

My technical strength on G1 taps off John Cuthbertson, and I am thankful to him for supporting my crazy queries and patiently listening and working with me to "make G1 adaptive" and to "tame mixed collections." When we used to discuss the adaptive marking threshold, I got tired of typing and talking about `InitiatingHeapOccupancyPercent`, so I shortened it to IHOP and John just loved it. It's really hard to find such supportive colleagues as John and Charlie.

And then there are Paul Hohensee and Tony Printezis. They are my mentors in their own right, and I can assure you that their persistence in reviewing my chapters has improved the readability and content by at least 75 percent! :)

Thank you all for trusting me and encouraging me. I am forever in your debt!

Poonam Parhar

I was deeply honored and excited when Charlie suggested that I write a chapter on the Serviceability Agent. I thought it was a great idea, as this wonderful tool is little known to the world, and it would be great to talk about its usefulness and capabilities. But I had never written a book before, and I was nervous. Big thanks to Charlie for his trust in me, for his encouragement, and for guiding me throughout writing the chapter on the SA.

I would like to thank my manager, Mattis Castegren, for always being supportive and encouraging of my work on this book, and for being the first reviewer of the chapter on the SA. Huge thanks to Kevin Walls for reviewing my chapter and helping me improve the quality of the content.

Special thanks to my husband, Onkar, who is my best friend, too, for being supportive and always being there whenever I need help. And of course I am grateful to my two little angels, Amanvir and Karanvir, who are my continuous source of motivation and happiness.

And my most sincere thanks to my father, Subhash C. Bajaj, for his infectious cheerfulness and for being a source of light, and for always inspiring me to never give up.

Bengt Rutisson

When Charlie asked me to write a chapter for this book, I was very honored and flattered. I had never written a book before and clearly had no idea how much work it is—even to write just one chapter! I am very grateful for all the support from Charlie and the reviewers. Without their help, I would not have been able to complete this chapter.

A big thanks to my wife, Sara Fritzell, who encouraged me throughout the work and helped me set up deadlines to get the chapter completed. And, of course, many thanks to our children, Max, Elsa, Teo, Emil, and Lina, for putting up with me during the writing period.

I would also like to thank all of the members of the HotSpot GC engineering team, both past and present. They are by far the most talented bunch of engineers I have ever worked with. I have learned so much from all of them, and they have all inspired me in so many ways.

About the Authors

Charlie Hunt (Chicago, IL) is currently a JVM Engineer at Oracle leading a variety of Java SE and HotSpot VM projects whose primary focus is reducing memory footprint while maintaining throughput and latency. He is also the lead author of *Java™ Performance* (Addison-Wesley, 2012). He is a regular presenter at the JavaOne Conference where he has been recognized as a Java Rock Star. He has also been a speaker at other well-known conferences, including QCon, Velocity, GoTo, and Dreamforce. Prior to leading a variety of Java SE and HotSpot VM projects for Oracle, Charlie worked in several different performance positions, including Performance Engineering Architect at Salesforce.com and HotSpot VM Performance Architect at Oracle and Sun Microsystems. He wrote his first Java application in 1998, joined Sun Microsystems in 1999 as Senior Java Architect, and has had a passion for Java and JVM performance ever since.

Monica Beckwith is an Independent Performance Consultant optimizing customer applications for server-class systems running the Java Virtual Machine. Her past experiences include working with Oracle, Sun Microsystems, and AMD. Monica has worked with Java HotSpot VM optimizing the JIT compiler, the generated code, the JVM heuristics, and garbage collection and collectors. She is a regular speaker at various conferences and has several published articles on topics including garbage collection, the Java memory model, and others. Monica led Oracle's Garbage First Garbage Collector performance team, and was named a JavaOne Rock Star.

Poonam Parhar (Santa Clara, CA) is currently a JVM Sustaining Engineer at Oracle where her primary responsibility is to resolve customer-escalated problems against JRockit and HotSpot VMs. She loves debugging and troubleshooting problems and is always focused on improving the serviceability and supportability of the HotSpot VM. She has nailed down many complex garbage collection issues in the HotSpot VM and is passionate about improving the debugging tools and the serviceability of the product so as to make it easier to troubleshoot and fix garbage-collector-related issues in the HotSpotVM. She has made several contributions to the Serviceability Agent debugger and also developed a VisualVM plugin for it. She presented "VisualVM Plugin for the SA" at the JavaOne 2011 conference. In an attempt to help customers and the Java community, she shares her work experiences and knowledge through the blog she maintains at https://blogs.oracle.com/poonam/.

Bengt Rutisson (Stockholm, Sweden) is a JVM Engineer at Oracle, working on the HotSpot engineering team. He has worked on garbage collectors in JVMs for the past 10 years, first with the JRockit VM and the last six years with the HotSpot VM. Bengt is an active participant in the OpenJDK project, with many contributions of features, stability fixes, and performance enhancements.

Garbage First Overview

This chapter is an introduction to the Garbage First (or G1) garbage collector (GC) along with a historical perspective on the garbage collectors in the Java HotSpot Virtual Machine (VM), hereafter called just HotSpot, and the reasoning behind G1's inclusion in HotSpot. The reader is assumed to be familiar with basic garbage collection concepts such as young generation, old generation, and compaction. Chapter 3, "JVM Overview," of the book *Java™ Performance* [1] is a good source for learning more about these concepts.

Serial GC was the first garbage collector introduced in HotSpot in 1999 as part of Java Development Kit (JDK) 1.3.1. The Parallel and Concurrent Mark Sweep collectors were introduced in 2002 as part of JDK 1.4.2. These three collectors roughly correspond to the three most important GC use cases: "minimize memory footprint and concurrent overhead," "maximize application throughput," and "minimize GC-related pause times." One might ask, "Why do we need a new collector such as G1?" Before answering, let's clarify some terminology that is often used when comparing and contrasting garbage collectors. We'll then move on to a brief overview of the four HotSpot garbage collectors, including G1, and identify how G1 differs from the others.

Terminology

In this section, we define the terms *parallel*, *stop-the-world*, and *concurrent*. The term *parallel* means a multithreaded garbage collection operation. When a GC event activity is described as parallel, multiple threads are used to perform it. When a garbage collector is described as parallel, it uses multiple threads to perform garbage collection. In the case of the HotSpot garbage collectors, almost all multithreaded GC operations are handled by internal Java VM (JVM) threads. One major exception to this is the G1 garbage collector, in which some background GC work can be taken on by the application threads. For more detail see Chapter 2, "Garbage First Garbage Collector in Depth," and Chapter 3, "Garbage First Garbage Collector Performance Tuning."

The term *stop-the-world* means that all Java application threads are stopped during a GC event. A stop-the-world garbage collector is one that stops all Java application threads when it performs a garbage collection. A GC phase or event may be described as stop-the-world, which means that during that particular GC phase or event all Java application threads are stopped.

The term *concurrent* means that garbage collection activity is occurring at the same time as the Java application is executing. A concurrent GC phase or event means that the GC phase or event executes at the same time as the application.

A garbage collector may be described by any one or a combination of these three terms. For example, a parallel concurrent collector is multithreaded (the parallel part) and also executes at the same time as the application (the concurrent part).

Parallel GC

Parallel GC is a parallel stop-the-world collector, which means that when a GC occurs, it stops all application threads and performs the GC work using multiple threads. The GC work can thus be done very efficiently without any interruptions. This is normally the best way to minimize the total time spent doing GC work relative to application work. However, individual pauses of the Java application induced by GC can be fairly long.

Both the young and old generation collections in Parallel GC are parallel and stop-the-world. Old generation collections also perform compaction. Compaction moves objects closer together to eliminate wasted space between them, leading to an optimal heap layout. However, compaction may take a considerable amount of time, which is generally a function of the size of the Java heap and the number and size of live objects in the old generation.

At the time when Parallel GC was introduced in HotSpot, only the young generation used a parallel stop-the-world collector. Old generation collections used a single-threaded stop-the-world collector. Back when Parallel GC was first introduced, the HotSpot command-line option that enabled Parallel GC in this configuration was `-XX:+UseParallelGC`.

At the time when Parallel GC was introduced, the most common use case for servers required throughput optimization, and hence Parallel GC became the default collector for the HotSpot Server VM. Additionally, the sizes of most Java heaps tended to be between 512MB and 2GB, which keeps Parallel GC pause times relatively low, even for single-threaded stop-the-world collections. Also at the time, latency requirements tended to be more relaxed than they are today. It was common for Web applications to tolerate GC-induced latencies in excess of one second, and as much as three to five seconds.

As Java heap sizes and the number and size of live objects in old generation grew, the time to collect the old generation became longer and longer. At the same time, hardware advances made more hardware threads available. As a result, Parallel GC was enhanced by adding a multithreaded old generation collector to be used with a multithreaded young generation collector. This enhanced Parallel GC reduced the time required to collect and compact the heap.

The enhanced Parallel GC was delivered in a Java 6 update release. It was enabled by a new command-line option called -XX:+UseParallelOldGC. When -XX:+UseParallelOldGC is enabled, parallel young generation collection is also enabled. This is what we think of today as Parallel GC in HotSpot, a multithreaded stop-the-world young generation collector combined with a multithreaded stop-the-world old generation collector.

Tip

In Java 7 update release 4 (also referred to as Java 7u4, or JDK 7u4), -XX:+UseParallelOldGC was made the default GC and the normal mode of operation for Parallel GC. As of Java 7u4, specifying -XX:+UseParallelGC also enables -XX:+UseParallelOldGC, and likewise specifying -XX:+UseParallelOldGC also enables -XX:+UseParallelGC.

Parallel GC is a good choice in the following use cases:

1. Application throughput requirements are much more important than latency requirements.

   A batch processing application is a good example since it is noninteractive. When you start a batch execution, you expect it to run to completion as fast as possible.

2. If worst-case application latency requirements can be met, Parallel GC will offer the best throughput. Worst-case latency requirements include both worst-case pause times, and also how frequently the pauses occur. For example, an application may have a latency requirement of "pauses that exceed 500ms shall not occur more than once every two hours, and all pauses shall not exceed three seconds."

   An interactive application with a sufficiently small live data size such that a Parallel GC's full GC event is able to meet or beat worst-case GC-induced latency requirements for the application is a good example that fits this use case. However, since the amount of live data tends to be highly correlated with the size of the Java heap, the types of applications falling into this category are limited.

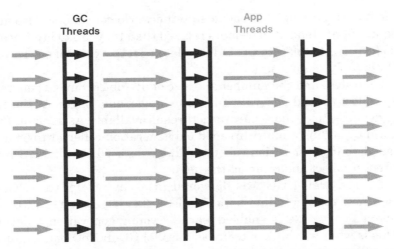

Figure 1.1 How Java application threads are interrupted by GC threads
when Parallel GC is used

Parallel GC works well for applications that meet these requirements. For applications that do not meet these requirements, pause times can become excessively long, since a full GC must mark through the entire Java heap and also compact the old generation space. As a result, pause times tend to increase with increased Java heap sizes.

Figure 1.1 illustrates how the Java application threads (gray arrows) are stopped and the GC threads (black arrows) take over to do the garbage collection work. In this diagram there are eight parallel GC threads and eight Java application threads, although in most applications the number of application threads usually exceeds the number of GC threads, especially in cases where some application threads may be idle. When a GC occurs, all application threads are stopped, and multiple GC threads execute during GC.

Serial GC

Serial GC is very similar to Parallel GC except that it does all its work in a single thread. The single-threaded approach allows for a less complex GC implementation and requires very few external runtime data structures. The memory footprint is the lowest of all HotSpot collectors. The challenges with Serial GC are similar to those for Parallel GC. Pause times can be long, and they grow more or less linearly with the heap size and amount of live data. In addition, with Serial GC the long pauses are more pronounced, since the GC work is done in a single thread.

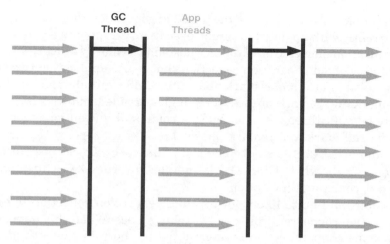

Figure 1.2 How Java application threads are interrupted by a single GC thread when Serial GC is used

Because of the low memory footprint, Serial GC is the default on the Java HotSpot Client VM. It also addresses the requirements for many embedded use cases. Serial GC can be explicitly specified as the GC to use with the `-XX:+UseSerialGC` HotSpot command-line option.

Figure 1.2 illustrates how Java application threads (gray arrows) are stopped and a single GC thread (black arrow) takes over to do the garbage collection work on a machine running eight Java application threads. Because it is single-threaded, Serial GC in most cases will take longer to execute a GC event than Parallel GC since Parallel GC can spread out the GC work to multiple threads.

Concurrent Mark Sweep (CMS) GC

CMS GC was developed in response to an increasing number of applications that demand a GC with lower worst-case pause times than Serial or Parallel GC and where it is acceptable to sacrifice some application throughput to eliminate or greatly reduce the number of lengthy GC pauses.

In CMS GC, young garbage collections are similar to those of Parallel GC. They are parallel stop-the-world, meaning all Java application threads are paused during young garbage collections and the garbage collection work is performed by multiple threads. Note that you can configure CMS GC with a single-threaded young generation collector, but this option has been deprecated in Java 8 and is removed in Java 9.

The major difference between Parallel GC and CMS GC is the old generation collection. For CMS GC, the old generation collections attempt to avoid long pauses in application threads. To achieve this, the CMS old generation collector does most of its work concurrently with application thread execution, except for a few relatively short GC synchronization pauses. CMS is often referred to as mostly concurrent, since there are some phases of old generation collection that pause application threads. Examples are the initial-mark and remark phases. In CMS's initial implementation, both the initial-mark and remark phases were single-threaded, but they have since been enhanced to be multithreaded. The HotSpot command-line options to support multithreaded initial-mark and remark phases are -XX:+CMSParallelInitialMark Enabled and -XX:CMSParallelRemarkEnabled. These are automatically enabled by default when CMS GC is enabled by the -XX:+UseConcurrent MarkSweepGC command-line option.

It is possible, and quite likely, for a young generation collection to occur while an old generation concurrent collection is taking place. When this happens, the old generation concurrent collection is interrupted by the young generation collection and immediately resumes upon the latter's completion. The default young generation collector for CMS GC is commonly referred to as ParNew.

Figure 1.3 shows how Java application threads (gray arrows) are stopped for the young GCs (black arrows) and for the CMS initial-mark and remark phases, and old generation GC stop-the-world phases (also black arrows). An old generation collection in CMS GC begins with a stop-the-world initial-mark phase. Once initial mark completes, the concurrent marking phase begins where the Java application threads are allowed to execute concurrently with the CMS marking threads. In Figure 1.3, the concurrent marking threads are the first two longer black arrows, one on top of the other below the "Marking/Pre-cleaning" label. Once concurrent marking completes, concurrent pre-cleaning is executed by the CMS threads, as shown by the two shorter black arrows under the "Marking/Pre-cleaning" label. Note that if there are enough available hardware threads, CMS thread execution overhead will not have much effect on the performance of Java application threads. If, however, the hardware threads are saturated or highly utilized, CMS threads will compete for CPU cycles with Java application threads. Once concurrent pre-cleaning completes, the stop-the-world remark phase begins. The remark phase marks objects that may have been missed after the initial mark and while concurrent marking and concurrent pre-cleaning execute. After the remark phase completes, concurrent sweeping begins, which frees all dead object space.

One of the challenges with CMS GC is tuning it such that the concurrent work can complete before the application runs out of available Java heap space. Hence, one tricky part about CMS is to find the right time to start the concurrent work. A common consequence of the concurrent approach is that CMS normally requires on the order of 10 to 20 percent more Java heap space than Parallel GC to handle the same application. That is part of the price paid for shorter GC pause times.

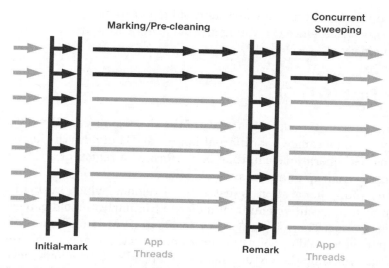

Figure 1.3 How Java application threads are impacted by the GC threads when CMS is used

Another challenge with CMS GC is how it deals with fragmentation in the old generation. Fragmentation occurs when the free space between objects in the old generation becomes so small or nonexistent that an object being promoted from the young generation cannot fit into an available hole. The CMS concurrent collection cycle does not perform compaction, not even incremental or partial compaction. A failure to find an available hole causes CMS to fall back to a full collection using Serial GC, typically resulting in a lengthy pause. Another unfortunate challenge associated with fragmentation in CMS is that it is unpredictable. Some application runs may never experience a full GC resulting from old generation fragmentation while others may experience it regularly.

Tuning CMS GC can help postpone fragmentation, as can application modifications such as avoiding large object allocations. Tuning can be a nontrivial task and requires much expertise. Making changes to the application to avoid fragmentation may also be challenging.

Summary of the Collectors

All of the collectors described thus far have some common issues. One is that the old generation collectors must scan the entire old generation for most of their operations such as marking, sweeping, and compacting. This means that the time to perform the work scales more or less linearly with the Java heap size. Another is that it must be decided up front where the young and old generations should be placed in the virtual address space, since the young and old generations are separate consecutive chunks of memory.

Garbage First (G1) GC

The G1 garbage collector addresses many of the shortcomings of Parallel, Serial, and CMS GC by taking a somewhat different approach. G1 divides the heap into a set of regions. Most GC operations can then be performed a region at a time rather than on the entire Java heap or an entire generation.

In G1, the young generation is just a set of regions, which means that it is not required to be a consecutive chunk of memory. Similarly, the old generation is also just a set of regions. There is no need to decide at JVM launch time which regions should be part of the old or young generation. In fact, the normal operational state for G1 is that over time the virtual memory mapped to G1 regions moves back and forth between the generations. A G1 region may be designated as young and later, after a young generation collection, become available for use elsewhere, since young generation regions are completely evacuated to unused regions.

In the remainder of this chapter, the term *available region* is used to identify regions that are unused and available for use by G1. An available region can be used or designated as a young or old generation region. It is possible that after a young generation collection, a young generation region can at some future time be used as an old generation region. Likewise, after collection of an old generation region, it becomes an available region that can at some future time be used as a young generation region.

G1 young collections are parallel stop-the-world collections. As mentioned earlier, parallel stop-the-world collections pause all Java application threads while the garbage collector threads execute, and the GC work is spread across multiple threads. As with the other HotSpot garbage collectors, when a young generation collection occurs, the entire young generation is collected.

Old generation G1 collections are quite different from those of the other HotSpot collectors. G1 old generation collections do not require the entire old generation to be collected in order to free space in the old generation. Instead, only a subset of the old generation regions may be collected at any one time. In addition, this subset of old generation regions is collected in conjunction with a young collection.

> **Tip**
>
> The term to describe the collection of a subset of old generation regions in conjunction with a young collection is *mixed GC*. Hence, a mixed GC is a GC event in which all young generation regions are collected in addition to a subset of old generation regions. In other words, a mixed GC is a mix of young and old generation regions that are being collected.

Similar to CMS GC, there is a fail-safe to collect and compact the entire old generation in dire situations such as when old generation space is exhausted.

A G1 old generation collection, ignoring the fail-safe type of collection, is a set of phases, some of which are parallel stop-the-world and some of which are parallel concurrent. That is, some phases are multithreaded and stop all application threads, and others are multithreaded and execute at the same time as the application threads. Chapters 2 and 3 provide more detail on each of these phases.

G1 initiates an old generation collection when a Java heap occupancy threshold is exceeded. It is important to note that the heap occupancy threshold in G1 measures the old generation occupancy compared to the entire Java heap. Readers who are familiar with CMS GC remember that CMS initiates an old generation collection using an occupancy threshold applied against the old generation space only. In G1, once the heap occupancy threshold is reached or exceeded, a parallel stop-the-world initial-mark phase is scheduled to execute.

The initial-mark phase executes at the same time as the next young GC. Once the initial-mark phase completes, a concurrent multithreaded marking phase is initiated to mark all live objects in the old generation. When the concurrent marking phase is completed, a parallel stop-the-world remark phase is scheduled to mark any objects that may have been missed due to application threads executing concurrently with the marking phase. At the end of the remark phase, G1 has full marking information on the old generation regions. If there happen to be old generation regions that do not have any live objects in them, they can be reclaimed without any additional GC work during the next phase of the concurrent cycle, the cleanup phase.

Also at the end of the remark phase, G1 can identify an optimal set of old generations to collect.

Tip

The set of regions to collect during a garbage collection is referred to as a collection set (CSet).

The regions selected for inclusion in a CSet are based on how much space can be freed and the G1 pause time target. After the CSet has been identified, G1 schedules a GC to collect regions in the CSet during the next several young generation GCs. That is, over the next several young GCs, a portion of the old generation will be collected in addition to the young generation. This is the mixed GC type of garbage collection event mentioned earlier.

With G1, every region that is garbage collected, regardless of whether it is young or old generation, has its live objects evacuated to an available region. Once the live objects have been evacuated, the young and/or old regions that have been collected become available regions.

An attractive outcome of evacuating live objects from old generation regions into available regions is that the evacuated objects end up next to each other in the virtual address space. There is no fragmented empty space between objects. Effectively, G1 does partial compaction of the old generation. Remember that CMS, Parallel, and Serial GC all require a full GC to compact the old generation and that compaction scans the entire old generation.

Since G1 performs GC operations on a per-region basis, it is suitable for large Java heaps. The amount of GC work can be limited to a small set of regions even though the Java heap size may be rather large.

The largest contributors to pause times in G1 are young and mixed collections, so one of the design goals of G1 is to allow the user to set a GC pause time goal. G1 attempts to meet the specified pause time goal through adaptive sizing of the Java heap. It will automatically adjust the size of the young generation and the total Java heap size based on the pause time goal. The lower the pause time goal, the smaller the young generation and the larger the total heap size, making the old generation relatively large.

A G1 design goal is to limit required tuning to setting a maximum Java heap size and specifying a GC pause time target. Otherwise, G1 is designed to dynamically tune itself using internal heuristics. At the time of writing, the heuristics within G1 are where most active HotSpot GC development is taking place. Also as of this writing, G1 may require additional tuning in some cases, but the prerequisites to building good heuristics are present and look promising. For advice on how to tune G1, see Chapter 3.

To summarize, G1 scales better than the other garbage collectors for large Java heaps by splitting the Java heap into regions. G1 deals with Java heap fragmentation with the help of partial compactions, and it does almost all its work in a multithreaded fashion.

As of this writing, G1 primarily targets the use case of large Java heaps with reasonably low pauses, and also those applications that are using CMS GC. There are plans to use G1 to also target the throughput use case, but for applications looking for high throughput that can tolerate longer GC pauses, Parallel GC is currently the better choice.

G1 Design

As mentioned earlier, G1 divides the Java heap into regions. The region size can vary depending on the size of the heap but must be a power of 2 and at least 1MB and at most 32MB. Possible region sizes are therefore 1, 2, 4, 8, 16, and 32MB. All regions are the same size, and their size does not change during execution of the JVM. The region size calculation is based on the average of the initial and maximum Java heap sizes such that there are about 2000 regions for that average heap size. As an example, for a 16GB Java heap with -Xmx16g -Xms16g command-line options, G1 will choose a region size of 16GB/2000 = 8MB.

If the initial and maximum Java heap sizes are far apart or if the heap size is very large, it is possible to have many more than 2000 regions. Similarly, a small heap size may end up with many fewer than 2000 regions.

Each region has an associated remembered set (a collection of the locations that contain pointers into the region, shortened to RSet). The total RSet size is limited but noticeable, so the number of regions has a direct effect on HotSpot's memory footprint. The total size of the RSets heavily depends on application behavior. At the low end, RSet overhead is around 1 percent and at the high end 20 percent of the heap size.

A particular region is used for only one purpose at a time, but when the region is included in a collection, it will be completely evacuated and released as an available region.

There are several types of regions in G1. Available regions are currently unused. Eden regions constitute the young generation eden space, and survivor regions constitute the young generation survivor space. The set of all eden and survivor regions together is the young generation. The number of eden or survivor regions can change from one GC to the next, between young, mixed, or full GCs. Old generation regions comprise most of the old generation. Finally, humongous regions are considered to be part of the old generation and contain objects whose size is 50 percent or more of a region. Until a JDK 8u40 change, humongous regions were collected as part of the old generation, but in JDK 8u40 certain humongous regions are collected as part of a young collection. There is more detail on humongous regions later in this chapter.

The fact that a region can be used for any purpose means that there is no need to partition the heap into contiguous young and old generation segments. Instead, G1 heuristics estimate how many regions the young generation can consist of and still be collected within a given GC pause time target. As the application starts allocating objects, G1 chooses an available region, designates it as an eden region, and starts handing out memory chunks from it to Java threads. Once the region is full, another unused region is designated an eden region. The process continues until the maximum number of eden regions is reached, at which point a young GC is initiated.

During a young GC, all young regions, eden and survivor, are collected. All live objects in those regions are evacuated to either a new survivor region or to an old generation region. Available regions are tagged as survivor or old generation regions as needed when the current evacuation target region becomes full.

When the occupancy of the old generation space, after a GC, reaches or exceeds the initiating heap occupancy threshold, G1 initiates an old generation collection. The occupancy threshold is controlled by the command-line option -XX:InitiatingHeapOccupancyPercent, which defaults to 45 percent of the Java heap.

G1 can reclaim old generation regions early when the marking phase shows that they contain no live objects. Such regions are added to the available region set. Old regions containing live objects are scheduled to be included in a future mixed collection.

G1 uses multiple concurrent marking threads. In an attempt to avoid stealing too much CPU from application threads, marking threads do their work in bursts. They do as much work as they can fit into a given time slot and then pause for a while, allowing the Java threads to execute instead.

Humongous Objects

G1 deals specially with large object allocations, or what G1 calls "humongous objects." As mentioned earlier, a humongous object is an object that is 50 percent or more of a region size. That size includes the Java object header. Object header sizes vary between 32- and 64-bit HotSpot VMs. The header size for a given object within a given HotSpot VM can be obtained using the Java Object Layout tool, also known as JOL. As of this writing, the Java Object Layout tool can be found on the Internet [2].

When a humongous object allocation occurs, G1 locates a set of consecutive available regions that together add up to enough memory to contain the humongous object. The first region is tagged as a "humongous start" region and the other regions are marked as "humongous continues" regions. If there are not enough consecutive available regions, G1 will do a full GC to compact the Java heap.

Humongous regions are considered part of the old generation, but they contain only one object. This property allows G1 to eagerly collect a humongous region when the concurrent marking phase detects that it is no longer live. When this happens, all the regions containing the humongous object can be reclaimed at once.

A potential challenge for G1 is that short-lived humongous objects may not be reclaimed until well past the point at which they become unreferenced. JDK 8u40 implemented a method to, in some cases, reclaim a humongous region during a young collection. Avoiding frequent humongous object allocations can be crucial to achieving application performance goals when using G1. The enhancements available in JDK 8u40 help but may not be a solution for all applications having many short-lived humongous objects.

Full Garbage Collections

Full GCs in G1 are implemented using the same algorithm as the Serial GC collector. When a full GC occurs, a full compaction of the entire Java heap is performed. This ensures that the maximum amount of free memory is available to the system. It is important to note that full GCs in G1 are single-threaded and as a result may introduce exceptionally long pause times. Also, G1 is designed such that full GCs are not expected to be necessary. G1 is expected to satisfy application performance goals without requiring a full GC and can usually be tuned such that a full GC is not needed.

Concurrent Cycle

A G1 concurrent cycle includes the activity of several phases: initial marking, concurrent root region scanning, concurrent marking, remarking, and cleanup. The beginning of a concurrent cycle is the initial mark, and the ending phase is cleanup. All these phases are considered part of "marking the live object graph" with the exception of the cleanup phase.

The purpose of the initial-mark phase is to gather all GC roots. Roots are the starting points of the object graphs. To collect root references from application threads, the application threads must be stopped; thus the initial-mark phase is stop-the-world. In G1, the initial marking is done as part of a young GC pause since a young GC must gather all roots anyway.

The marking operation must also scan and follow all references from objects in the survivor regions. This is what the concurrent root region scanning phase does. During this phase all Java threads are allowed to execute, so no application pauses occur. The only limitation is that the scanning must be completed before the next GC is allowed to start. The reason for that is that a new GC will generate a new set of survivor objects that are different from the initial mark's survivor objects.

Most marking work is done during the concurrent marking phase. Multiple threads cooperate to mark the live object graph. All Java threads are allowed to execute at the same time as the concurrent marking threads, so there is no pause in the application, though an application may experience some throughput reduction.

After concurrent marking is done, another stop-the-world phase is needed to finalize all marking work. This phase is called the "remark phase" and is usually a very short stop-the-world pause.

The final phase of concurrent marking is the cleanup phase. In this phase, regions that were found not to contain any live objects are reclaimed. These regions are not included in a young or mixed GC since they contain no live objects. They are added to the list of available regions.

The marking phases must be completed in order to find out what objects are live so as to make informed decisions about what regions to include in the mixed GCs. Since it is the mixed GCs that are the primary mechanism for freeing up memory in G1, it is important that the marking phase finishes before G1 runs out of available regions. If the marking phase does not finish prior to running out of available regions, G1 will fall back to a full GC to free up memory. This is reliable but slow. Ensuring that the marking phases complete in time to avoid a full GC may require tuning, which is covered in detail in Chapter 3.

Heap Sizing

The Java heap size in G1 is always a multiple of the region size. Except for that limitation, G1 can grow and shrink the heap size dynamically between -Xms and -Xmx just as the other HotSpot GCs do.

G1 may increase the Java heap size for several reasons:

1. An increase in size can occur based on heap size calculations during a full GC.

2. When a young or mixed GC occurs, G1 calculates the time spent to perform the GC compared to the time spent executing the Java application. If too much time is spent in GC according to the command-line setting -XX:GCTimeRatio, the Java heap size is increased. The idea behind growing the Java heap size in this situation is to allow GCs to happen less frequently so that the time spent in GC compared to the time spent executing the application is reduced.

   The default value for -XX:GCTimeRatio in G1 is 9. All other HotSpot garbage collectors default to a value of 99. The larger the value for GCTimeRatio, the more aggressive the increase in Java heap size. The other HotSpot collectors are thus more aggressive in their decision to increase Java heap size and by default are targeted to spend less time in GC relative to the time spent executing the application.

3. If an object allocation fails, even after having done a GC, rather than immediately falling back to doing a full GC, G1 will attempt to increase the heap size to satisfy the object allocation.

4. If a humongous object allocation fails to find enough consecutive free regions to allocate the object, G1 will try to expand the Java heap to obtain more available regions rather than doing a full GC.

5. When a GC requests a new region into which to evacuate objects, G1 will prefer to increase the size of the Java heap to obtain a new region rather than failing the GC and falling back to a full GC in an attempt to find an available region.

References

[1] Charlie Hunt and Binu John. *Java™ Performance*. Addison-Wesley, Upper Saddle River, NJ, 2012. ISBN 978-0-13-714252-1.

[2] "Code Tools: jol." OpenJDK, circa 2014. http://openjdk.java.net/projects/code-tools/jol/.

2

Garbage First Garbage Collector in Depth

This chapter aims at providing in-depth knowledge on the principles supporting HotSpot's latest garbage collector: the Garbage First garbage collector (referred to as G1 GC for short). These principles were highlighted in Chapter 1, "Garbage First Overview."

At various points during the narration, concepts like the collection cycles, internal structures, and algorithms will be introduced, followed by comprehensive details. The aim is to document the details without overloading the uninitiated.

To gain the most from the chapter, the reader is expected to be familiar with basic garbage collection concepts and terms and generally how garbage collection works in the Java HotSpot JVM. These concepts and terms include generational garbage collection, the Java heap, young generation space, old generation space, eden space, survivor space, parallel garbage collection, stop-the-world garbage collection, concurrent garbage collection, incremental garbage collection, marking, and compaction. Chapter 1 covers some of these concepts and terms. A good source for additional details is the "HotSpot VM Garbage Collectors" section in Chapter 3, "JVM Overview," of *Java™ Performance* [1].

Background

G1 GC is the latest addition to the Java HotSpot Virtual Machine. It is a compacting collector based on the principle of collecting the most garbage first, hence the name "Garbage First" GC. G1 GC has incremental, parallel, stop-the-world pauses that achieve compaction via copying and also has parallel, multistaged concurrent marking that helps in reducing the mark, remark, and cleanup pauses to a bare minimum.

With the introduction of G1 GC, HotSpot JVM moved from the conventional heap layout where the generations are contiguous to generations that are now composed of noncontiguous heap regions. Thus, for an active Java heap, a particular region could be a part of either eden or survivor or old generation, or it could be a humongous region or even just a free region. Multiples of these regions form a "logical" generation to match conventional wisdom formed by previous HotSpot garbage collectors' idea of generational spaces.

Garbage Collection in G1

G1 GC reclaims most of its heap regions during collection pauses. The only exception to this is the cleanup stage of the multistaged concurrent marking cycle. During the cleanup stage, if G1 GC encounters purely garbage-filled regions, it can immediately reclaim those regions and return them to a linked list of free regions; thus, freeing up those regions does not have to wait for the next garbage collection pause.

G1 GC has three main types of garbage collection cycles: a young collection cycle, a multistage concurrent marking cycle, and a mixed collection cycle. There is also a single-threaded (as of this writing) fallback pause called a "full" garbage collection pause, which is the fail-safe mechanism for G1 GC in case the GC experiences evacuation failures.

> **Tip**
>
> An evacuation failure is also known as a promotion failure or to-space exhaustion or even to-space overflow. The failure usually happens when there is no more free space to promote objects. When faced with such a scenario, all Java HotSpot VM GCs try to expand their heaps. But if the heap is already at its maximum, the GC tries to tenure the regions where objects were successfully copied and update their references. For G1 GC, the objects that could not be copied are tenured in place. All GCs will then have their references self-forwarded. These self-forwarded references are removed at the end of the garbage collection cycle.

During a young collection, G1 GC pauses the application threads to move live objects from the young regions into survivor regions or promote them into old regions or both. For a mixed collection, G1 GC additionally moves live objects from the most (for lack of a better term) "efficient" old regions into free region(s), which become a part of the old generation.

> **Tip**
>
> "GC efficiency" actually refers to the ratio of the space to be reclaimed versus the estimated GC cost to collect the region. Due to the lack of a better term, in this book we refer to the sorting of the heap regions in order to identify candidate regions as calculating the "GC efficiency." The reason for using the same terminology is that GC efficiency evaluates the benefit of collecting a region with respect to the cost of collecting it. And the "efficiency" that we are referring to here is solely dependent on liveness accounting and hence is just the cost of collecting a region. For example, an old region whose collection is less time-consuming than other more expensive old regions is considered to be an "efficient" region. The most efficient regions would be the first ones in the sorted array of regions.

At the end of a collection cycle, the regions that were a part of the collection set or CSet (refer to the section "Collection Sets and Their Importance" later in this chapter for more information) are guaranteed to be free and are returned to the free list. Let's talk about these concepts in more detail.

The Young Generation

G1 GC is a generational GC comprising the young generation and the old generation. Most allocations, with a few exceptions such as objects too large to fit in the allocating thread's local allocation buffer (also known as a TLAB) but smaller than what would be considered "humongous," and of course the "humongous" objects themselves (see the section "Humongous Regions" for more information), by any particular thread will land in that thread's TLAB. A TLAB enables faster allocations since the owning Java thread is able to allocate in a lock-free manner. These TLABs are from G1 regions that become a part of the young generation. Unless explicitly specified on the command line, the current young generation size is calculated based on the initial and maximum young generation size bounds (as of JDK 8u45 the defaults are 5 percent of the total Java heap for initial young generation size (`-XX:G1NewSizePercent`) and 60 percent of the total Java heap for maximum young generation size (`-XX:G1MaxNewSizePercent`) and the pause time goal of the application (`-XX:MaxGCPauseMillis`).

> **Tip**
>
> G1 GC will select the default of 200ms if `-XX:MaxGCPauseMillis` is not set on the command line. If the user sets `-Xmn` or related young generation sizing command-line options such as `-XX:NewRatio`, G1 GC may not be able to adjust the young generation size based on the pause time goal, and hence the pause time target could become a moot option.

Based on the Java application's object allocation rate, new free regions are added to the young generation as needed until the desired generation size is met. The heap region size is determined at the launch of the JVM. The heap region size has to be a power of 2 and can range anywhere from 1MB to 32MB. The JVM shoots for approximately 2048 regions and sets the heap region size accordingly (Heap region size = Heap size/2048). The heap region size is aligned and adjusted to fall within the 1MB to 32MB and power of 2 bounds. The adaptive selection of heap region size can be overwritten on the command line by setting it with `-XX:G1HeapRegionSize=n`. Chapter 3, "Garbage First Garbage Collector Performance Tuning," includes more information on when to override the JVM's automatic sizing.

A Young Collection Pause

The young generation consists of G1 GC regions designated as eden regions and G1 GC regions designated as survivor regions. A young collection is triggered when the JVM fails to allocate out of the eden region, that is, the eden is completely filled. The GC then steps in to free some space. The first young collection will move all the live objects from the eden regions into the survivor regions. This is known as "copy to survivor." From then on, any young collection will promote the live objects from the entire young generation (i.e., eden and survivor regions) into new regions that are now the new survivor regions. The young collections will also occasionally promote a few objects into regions out of the old generation when they survive a predetermined promotion threshold. This is called "aging" the live objects. The promotion of the live objects from the young generation into the old generation is called "tenuring" the objects, and consequently the age threshold is called the "tenuring threshold." The promotion of objects into the survivor regions or into the old generation happens in the promoting GC thread's local allocation buffer (also known as Promotion Lab, or PLAB for short). There is a per-GC-thread PLAB for the survivor regions and for the old generation.

During every young collection pause, G1 GC calculates the amount of expansion or contraction to be performed on the current young generation size (i.e., G1 GC decides to either add or remove free regions) based on the total time that it took to perform the current collection; the size of the remembered sets or RSets (more on this in the section "Remembered Sets and Their Importance" later in this chapter); the current, the maximum, and the minimum young generation capacity; and the pause time target. Thus the young generation is resized at the end of a collection pause. The previous and the next sizes of the young generation can be observed and calculated by looking at the output of `-XX:+PrintGCDetails`. Let's look at an example. (Note that throughout this book lines of output have been wrapped in order to fit on the book page.)

```
15.894: [GC pause (G1 Evacuation Pause) (young), 0.0149364 secs]
    [Parallel Time: 9.8 ms, GC Workers: 8]
<snip>
    [Code Root Fixup: 0.1 ms]
    [Code Root Purge: 0.0 ms]
    [Clear CT: 0.2 ms]
    [Other: 4.9 ms]
<snip>
[Eden: 695.0M(695.0M)->0.0B(1043.0M) Survivors: 10.0M->13.0M Heap:
748.5M(1176.0M)->57.0M(1760.0M)]
    [Times: user=0.08 sys=0.00, real=0.01 secs]
```

Here the new size of the young generation can be calculated by adding the new Eden size to the new Survivors size (i.e., 1043M + 13M = 1056M).

Object Aging and the Old Generation

As was covered briefly in the previous section, "A Young Collection Pause," during every young collection, G1 GC maintains the age field per object. The current total number of young collections that any particular object survives is called the "age" of that object. The GC maintains the age information, along with the total size of the objects that have been promoted into that age, in a table called the "age table." Based on the age table, the survivor size, the survivor fill capacity (determined by the -XX:TargetSurvivorRatio (default = 50)), and the -XX:MaxTenuringThreshold (default = 15), the JVM adaptively sets a tenuring threshold for all surviving objects. Once the objects cross this tenuring threshold, they get promoted/tenured into the old generation regions. When these tenured objects die in the old generation, their space can be freed by a mixed collection, or during cleanup (but only if the entire region can be reclaimed), or, as a last resort, during a full garbage collection.

Humongous Regions

For the G1 GC, the unit of collection is a region. Hence, the heap region size (-XX:G1HeapRegionSize) is an important parameter since it determines what size objects can fit into a region. The heap region size also determines what objects are characterized as "humongous." Humongous objects are very large objects that span 50 percent or more of a G1 GC region. Such an object doesn't follow the usual fast allocation path and instead gets allocated directly out of the old generation in regions marked as humongous regions.

Figure 2.1 illustrates a contiguous Java heap with the different types of G1 regions identified: young region, old region, and humongous region. Here, we can see that each of the young and old regions spans one unit of collection. The humongous region,

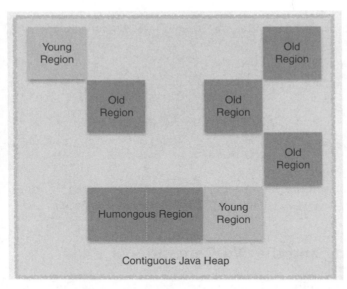

Figure 2.1 G1 Java heap layout

on the other hand, spans two units of collection, indicating that humongous regions are formed of contiguous heap regions. Let's look a little deeper into three different humongous regions.

In Figure 2.2, Humongous Object 1 spans two contiguous regions. The first contiguous region is labeled "StartsHumongous," and the consecutive contiguous region is labeled "ContinuesHumongous." Also illustrated in Figure 2.2, Humongous Object 2 spans three contiguous heap regions, and Humongous Object 3 spans just one region.

Tip

Past studies of these humongous objects have indicated that the allocations of such objects are rare and that the objects themselves are long-lived. Another good point to remember is that the humongous regions need to be contiguous (as shown in Figure 2.2). Hence it makes no sense to move them since there is no gain (no space reclamation), and it is very expensive since large memory copies are not trivial in expense. Hence, in an effort to avoid the copying expense of these humongous objects during young garbage collections, it was deemed better to directly allocate the humongous objects out of the old generation. But in recent years, there are many transaction-type applications that may have not-so-long-lived humongous objects. Hence, various efforts are being made to optimize the allocation and reclamation of humongous objects.

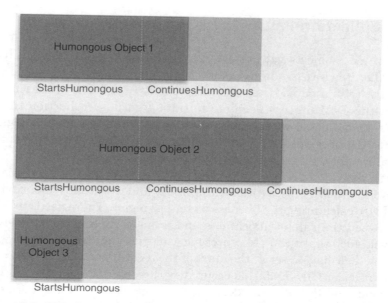

Figure 2.2 Differing humongous objects mapping to humongous regions

As mentioned earlier, humongous objects follow a separate and quite involved allocation path. This means the humongous object allocation path doesn't take advantage of any of the young generation TLABs and PLABs that are optimized for allocation or promotion, since the cost of zeroing the newly allocated object would be massive and probably would circumvent any allocation path optimization gain. Another noteworthy difference in the handling of humongous objects is in the collection of humongous regions. Prior to JDK 8u40, if any humongous region was completely free, it could be collected only during the cleanup pause of the concurrent collection cycle. In an effort to optimize the collection of short-lived humongous objects, JDK 8u40 made a noteworthy change such that if the humongous regions are determined to have no incoming references, they can be reclaimed and returned to the list of free regions during a young collection. A full garbage collection pause will also collect completely free humongous regions.

Tip

An important potential issue or confusion needs to be highlighted here. Say the current G1 region size is 2MB. And say that the length of a byte array is aligned at 1MB. This byte array will still be considered a humongous object and will need to be allocated as such, since the 1MB array length doesn't include the array's object header size.

A Mixed Collection Pause

As more and more objects get promoted into the old regions or when humongous objects get allocated into the humongous regions, the occupancy of the old generation and hence the total occupied Java heap increases. In order to avoid running out of heap space, the JVM process needs to initiate a garbage collection that not only covers the regions in the young generation but also adds some old regions to the mix. Refer to the previous section on humongous regions to read about the special handling (allocation and reclamation) of humongous objects.

In order to identify old regions with the most garbage, G1 GC initiates a concurrent marking cycle, which helps with marking roots and eventually identifying all live objects and also calculating the liveness factor per region. There needs to be a delicate balance between the rate of allocations and promotions and the triggering of this marking cycle such that the JVM process doesn't run out of Java heap space. Hence, an occupancy threshold is set at the start of the JVM process. As of this writing and up through at least JDK 8u45 this occupancy threshold is not adaptive and can be set by the command-line option `-XX:InitiatingHeapOccupancyPercent` (which I very fondly call IHOP).

Tip

In G1, the IHOP threshold defaults to 45 percent of the total Java heap. It is important to note that this heap occupancy percentage applies to the entire Java heap, unlike the heap occupancy command-line option used with CMS GC where it applies only to the old generation. In G1 GC, there is no physically separate old generation—there is a single pool of free regions that can be allocated as eden, survivor, old, or humongous. Also, the number of regions that are allocated, for say the eden, can vary over time. Hence having an old generation percentage didn't really make sense.

Trivia

I used to write e-mails to G1 GC dev engineers and also to G1 GC users about the marking threshold and would always have to refer to it in full as `InitiatingHeapOccupancyPercent` since there is another difference (other than the one mentioned in the preceding tip) between CMS and G1's marking threshold—it's the option name! CMS's marking threshold is called `CMSInitiatingOccupancyFraction`, and as you can see there is no "percent" in the option name. So to avoid any confusion, I would always have to specify the full option name for G1, and soon I developed a form of endearment for this option and started calling it IHOP.

When the old generation occupancy reaches (or exceeds) the IHOP threshold, a concurrent marking cycle is initiated. Toward the end of marking, G1 GC calculates the amount of live objects per old region. Also, during the cleanup stage, G1 GC ranks the old regions based on their "GC efficiency." Now a mixed collection can happen! During a mixed collection pause, G1 GC not only collects all of the regions in the young generation but also collects a few candidate old regions such that the old regions with the most garbage are reclaimed.

> **Tip**
>
> An important point to keep in mind when comparing CMS and G1 logs is that the multistaged concurrent cycle in G1 has fewer stages than the multistaged concurrent cycle in CMS.

A single mixed collection is similar to a young collection pause and achieves compaction of the live objects via copying. The only difference is that during a mixed collection, the collection set also incorporates a few efficient old regions. Depending on a few parameters (as discussed later in this chapter), there could be more than one mixed collection pause. This is called a "mixed collection cycle." A mixed collection cycle can happen only after the marking/IHOP threshold is crossed and after the completion of a concurrent marking cycle.

There are two important parameters that help determine the total number of mixed collections in a mixed collection cycle: `-XX:G1MixedGCCountTarget` and `-XX:G1HeapWastePercent`.

`-XX:G1MixedGCCountTarget`, which defaults to 8 (JDK 8u45), is the mixed GC count target option whose intent is to set a physical limit on the number of mixed collections that will happen after the marking cycle is complete. G1 GC divides the total number of candidate old regions available for collection by the count target number and sets that as the minimum number of old regions to be collected per mixed collection pause. This can be represented as an equation as follows:

Minimum old CSet per mixed collection pause = Total number of candidate old regions identified for mixed collection cycle/`G1MixedGCCountTarget`

`-XX:G1HeapWastePercent`, which defaults to 5 percent (JDK 8u45) of the total Java heap, is an important parameter that controls the number of old regions to be collected during a mixed collection cycle. For every mixed collection pause, G1 GC identifies the amount of reclaimable heap based on the dead object space that can be reclaimed. As soon as G1 GC reaches this heap waste threshold percentage, G1 GC stops the initiation of a mixed collection pause, thus culminating the mixed collection cycle. Setting the heap waste percent basically helps with limiting the amount of heap that you are willing to waste to effectively speed up the mixed collection cycle.

Thus the number of mixed collections per mixed collection cycle can be controlled by the minimum old generation CSet per mixed collection pause count and the heap waste percentage.

Collection Sets and Their Importance

During any garbage collection pause all the regions in the CSet are freed. A CSet is a set of regions that are targeted for reclamation during a garbage collection pause. All live objects in these candidate regions will be evacuated during a collection, and the regions will be returned to a list of free regions. During a young collection, the CSet can contain only young regions for collection. A mixed collection, on the other hand, will not only add all the young regions but also add some old candidate regions (based on their GC efficiency) to its CSet.

There are two important parameters that help with the selection of candidate old regions for the CSet of a mixed collection: `-XX:G1MixedGCLiveThresholdPercent` and `-XX:G1OldCSetRegionThresholdPercent`.

`-XX:G1MixedGCLiveThresholdPercent`, which defaults to 85 percent (JDK 8u45) of a G1 GC region, is a liveness threshold and a set limit to exclude the most expensive of old regions from the CSet of mixed collections. G1 GC sets a limit such that any old region that falls below this liveness threshold is included in the CSet of a mixed collection.

`-XX:G1OldCSetRegionThresholdPercent`, which defaults to 10 percent (JDK 8u45) of the total Java heap, sets the maximum limit on the number of old regions that can be collected per mixed collection pause. The threshold is dependent on the total Java heap available to the JVM process and is expressed as a percentage of the total Java heap. Chapter 3 covers a few examples to highlight the functioning of these thresholds.

Remembered Sets and Their Importance

A generational collector segregates objects in different areas in the heap according to the age of those objects. These different areas in the heap are referred to as the generations. The generational collector then can concentrate most of its collection effort on the most recently allocated objects because it expects to find most of them dead sooner rather than later. These generations in the heap can be collected independently. The independent collection helps lower the response times since the GC doesn't have to scan the entire heap, and also (e.g., in the case of copying generational collectors) older long-lived objects don't have to be copied back and forth, thus reducing the copying and reference updating overhead.

In order to facilitate the independence of collections, many garbage collectors maintain RSets for their generations. An RSet is a data structure that helps maintain and track references into its own unit of collection (which in G1 GC's case is a region), thus eliminating the need to scan the entire heap for such information. When G1 GC executes a stop-the-world collection (young or mixed), it scans through the RSets of regions contained in its CSet. Once the live objects in the region are moved, their incoming references are updated.

With G1 GC, during any young or mixed collection, the young generation is always collected in its entirety, eliminating the need to track references whose containing object resides in the young generation. This reduces the RSet overhead. Thus, G1 GC just needs to maintain the RSets in the following two scenarios:

- Old-to-young references—G1 GC maintains pointers from regions in the old generation into the young generation region. The young generation region is said to "own" the RSet and hence the region is said to be an RSet "owning" region.

- Old-to-old references—Here pointers from different regions in the old generation will be maintained in the RSet of the "owning" old generation region.

In Figure 2.3, we can see one young region (Region x) and two old regions (Region y and Region z). Region x has an incoming reference from Region z. This reference is noted in the RSet for Region x. We also observe that Region z has two incoming references, one from Region x and another from Region y. The RSet for Region z needs to note only the incoming reference from Region y and doesn't have to remember the reference from Region x, since, as explained earlier, young generation is always collected in its entirety. Finally, for Region y, we see an incoming reference from Region x, which is not noted in the RSet for Region y since Region x is a young region.

As shown in Figure 2.3, there is only one RSet per region. Depending on the application, it could be that a particular region (and thus its RSet) could be "popular" such that there could be many updates in the same region or even to the same location. This is not that uncommon in Java applications.

G1 GC has its way of handling such demands of popularity; it does so by changing the density of RSets. The density of RSets follows three levels of granularity, namely, sparse, fine, and coarse. For a popular region, the RSet would probably get coarsened to accommodate the pointers from various other regions. This will be reflected in the RSet scanning time for those regions. (Refer to Chapter 3 for more details on RSet scanning times.) Each of the three granular levels has a per-region-table (PRT) abstract housing for any particular RSet.

Since G1 GC regions are internally further divided into chunks, at the G1 GC region level the lowest granularity achievable is a 512-byte heap chunk called a "card" (refer to Figure 2.4). A global card table maintains all the cards.

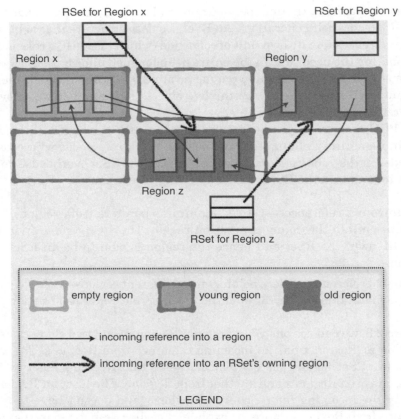

Figure 2.3 Remembered sets with incoming object references

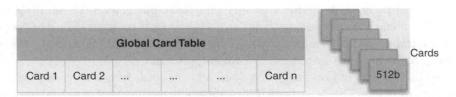

Figure 2.4 Global card table with 512-byte cards

When a pointer makes a reference to an RSet's owning region, the card containing that pointer is noted in the PRT. A sparse PRT is basically a hash table of those card indices. This simple implementation leads to faster scan times by the garbage collector. On the other hand, fine-grained PRT and coarse-grained bitmap are handled in a different manner. For fine-grained PRT, each entry in its open hash table corresponds to a region (with a reference into the owning region) where the card indices within that region are stored in a bitmap. There is a maximum limit to the fine-grained PRT, and when it is exceeded, a bit (called the "coarse-grained bit") is set in the coarse-grained bitmap. Once the coarse-grained bit is set, the corresponding entry in the fine-grained PRT is deleted. The coarse-grained bitmap is simply a bitmap with one bit per region such that a set bit means that the corresponding region might contain a reference to the owning region. So then the entire region associated with the set bit must be scanned to find the reference. Hence a remembered set coarsened to a coarse-grained bitmap is the slowest to scan for the garbage collector. More details on this can be found in Chapter 3.

During any collection cycle, when scanning the remembered sets and thus the cards in the PRT, G1 GC will mark the corresponding entry in the global card table to avoid rescanning that card. At the end of the collection cycle this card table is cleared; this is shown in the GC output (printed with `-XX:+PrintGCDetails`) as `Clear CT` and is next in sequence to the parallel work done by the GC threads (i.e., external root scanning, updating and scanning the remembered sets, object copying, and termination protocol). There are also other sequential activities such as choosing and freeing the CSet and also reference processing and enqueuing. Here is sample output using `-XX:+UseG1GC -XX:PrintGCDetails -XX:PrintGCTimeStamps` with build JDK 8u45. The RSet and card table activities are highlighted. More details on the output are covered in Chapter 3.

```
12.664: [GC pause (G1 Evacuation Pause) (young), 0.0010649 secs]
    [Parallel Time: 0.5 ms, GC Workers: 8]
        [GC Worker Start (ms): Min: 12664.1, Avg: 12664.2, Max:
12664.2, Diff: 0.1]
        [Ext Root Scanning (ms): Min: 0.2, Avg: 0.3, Max: 0.3, Diff:
0.1, Sum: 2.1]
        [Update RS (ms): Min: 0.0, Avg: 0.0, Max: 0.0, Diff: 0.0, Sum: 0.2]
            [Processed Buffers: Min: 1, Avg: 1.1, Max: 2, Diff: 1, Sum: 9]
        [Scan RS (ms): Min: 0.0, Avg: 0.0, Max: 0.0, Diff: 0.0, Sum: 0.1]
        [Code Root Scanning (ms): Min: 0.0, Avg: 0.0, Max: 0.0, Diff: 0.0,
Sum: 0.0]
        [Object Copy (ms): Min: 0.0, Avg: 0.0, Max: 0.1, Diff: 0.0,
Sum: 0.4]
        [Termination (ms): Min: 0.0, Avg: 0.0, Max: 0.0, Diff: 0.0,
Sum: 0.0]
        [GC Worker Other (ms): Min: 0.0, Avg: 0.0, Max: 0.0, Diff: 0.0,
Sum: 0.1]
        [GC Worker Total (ms): Min: 0.3, Avg: 0.4, Max: 0.4, Diff: 0.1,
Sum: 2.9]
        [GC Worker End (ms): Min: 12664.5, Avg: 12664.5, Max: 12664.5,
Diff: 0.0]
    [Code Root Fixup: 0.0 ms]
    [Code Root Purge: 0.0 ms]
```

Continued

```
[Clear CT: 0.1 ms]
[Other: 0.4 ms]
    [Choose CSet: 0.0 ms]
    [Ref Proc: 0.2 ms]
    [Ref Enq: 0.0 ms]
    [Redirty Cards: 0.1 ms]
    [Humongous Reclaim: 0.0 ms]
    [Free CSet: 0.1 ms]
  [Eden: 83.0M(83.0M)->0.0B(83.0M) Survivors: 1024.0K->1024.0K Heap:
104.0M(140.0M)->21.0M(140.0M)]
 [Times: user=0.00 sys=0.00, real=0.01 secs]
```

Concurrent Refinement Threads and Barriers

The advanced RSet structure comes with its own maintenance costs in the form of write barriers and concurrent "refinement" threads.

Barriers are snippets of native code that are executed when certain statements in a managed runtime are executed. The use of barriers in garbage collection algorithms is well established, and so is the cost associated with executing the barrier code since the native instruction path length increases.

OpenJDK HotSpot's Parallel Old and CMS GCs use a write barrier that executes when the HotSpot JVM performs an object reference write operation:

```
object.field = some_other_object;
```

The barrier updates a card-table-type structure [2] to track intergenerational references. The card table is scanned during minor garbage collections. The write barrier algorithm is based on Urs Hölzle's fast write barrier [3], which reduces the barrier overhead to just two extra instructions in the compiled code.

G1 GC employs a pre-write and a post-write barrier. The former is executed before the actual application assignment takes place and is covered in detail in the concurrent marking section, while the latter is executed after the assignment and is further described here.

G1 GC issues a write barrier anytime a reference is updated. For example, consider the update in this pseudo-code:

```
object.field = some_other_object;
```

This assignment will trigger the barrier code. Since the barrier is issued after a write to any reference, it is called a "post-write" barrier. Write barrier instruction sequences can get very expensive, and the throughput of the application will fall proportionally with the complexity of the barrier code; hence G1 GC does the minimum amount of work that is needed to figure out if the reference update is a cross-region update since a cross-region reference update needs to be captured in the RSet of the owning region. For G1 GC, the barrier code includes a filtering technique briefly discussed in "Older-First Garbage Collection in Practice" [4] that involves a simple check which evaluates to zero when the update is in the same region. The following pseudo-code illustrates G1 GC's write barrier:

```
(&object.field XOR &some_other_object) >> RegionSize
```

Anytime a cross-region update happens, G1 GC will enqueue the corresponding card in a buffer called the "update log buffer" or "dirty card queue." In our update example, the card containing object is logged in the update log buffer.

> **Tip**
>
> The concurrent refinement threads are threads dedicated to the sole purpose of maintaining the remembered sets by scanning the logged cards in the filled log buffers and then updating the remembered set for those regions. The maximum number of refinement threads is determined by -XX:G1ConcRefinementThreads. As of JDK 8u45, if -XX:G1ConcRefinementThreads is not set on the command line, it is ergonomically set to be the same as -XX:ParallelGCThreads.

Once the update log buffer reaches its holding capacity, it is retired and a new log buffer is allocated. The card enqueuing then happens in this new buffer. The retired buffer is placed in a global list. Once the refinement threads find entries in the global list, they start concurrently processing the retired buffers. The refinement threads are always active, albeit initially only a few of them are available. G1 GC handles the deployment of the concurrent refinement threads in a tiered fashion, adding more threads to keep up with the amount of filled log buffers. Activation thresholds are set by the following flags: -XX:G1ConcRefinementGreenZone, -XX:G1ConcRefinementYellowZone, and -XX:G1ConcRefinementRedZone. If the concurrent refinement threads can't keep up with the number of filled buffers, mutator threads are enlisted for help. At such a time, the mutator threads will stop their work and help the concurrent refinement threads to finish processing the filled log buffers. Mutator threads in GC terminology are the Java application threads. Hence, when the concurrent refinement threads can't keep up the number of filled buffers, the Java application will be halted until the filled log buffers are processed. Thus, measures should be taken to avoid such a scenario.

> **Tip**
>
> Users are not expected to manually tune any of the three refinement zones. There may be rare occasions when it makes sense to tune `-XX:G1ConcRefinementThreads` or `-XX:ParallelGCThreads`. Chapter 3 explains more about concurrent refinement and the refinement threads.

Concurrent Marking in G1 GC

With the introduction of G1 GC regions and liveness accounting per region, it became clear that an incremental and complete concurrent marking algorithm was required. Taiichi Yuasa presented an algorithm for incremental mark and sweep GC in which he employed a "snapshot-at-the-beginning" (SATB) marking algorithm [5].

Yuasa's SATB marking optimization concentrated on the concurrent marking phase of the mark-sweep GC. The SATB marking algorithm was well suited for G1 GC's regionalized heap structure and addressed a major complaint about the HotSpot JVM's CMS GC algorithm—the potential for lengthy remark pauses.

G1 GC establishes a marking threshold which is expressed as a percentage of the total Java heap and defaults to 45 percent. This threshold, which can be set at the command line using the `-XX:InitiatingHeapOccupancyPercent` (IHOP) option, when crossed, will initiate the concurrent marking cycle. The marking task is divided into chunks such that most of the work is done concurrently while the mutator threads are active. The goal is to have the entire Java heap marked before it reaches its full capacity.

The SATB algorithm simply creates an object graph that is a logical "snapshot" of the heap. SATB marking guarantees that all garbage objects that are present at the start of the concurrent marking phase will be identified by the snapshot. Objects allocated during the concurrent marking phase will be considered live, but they are not traced, thus reducing the marking overhead. The technique guarantees that all live objects that were alive at the start of the marking phase are marked and traced, and any new allocations made by the concurrent mutator threads during the marking cycle are marked as live and consequently not collected.

The marking data structures contain just two bitmaps: previous and next. The previous bitmap holds the last complete marking information. The current marking cycle creates and updates the next bitmap. As time passes, the previous marking information becomes more and more stale. Eventually, the next bitmap will replace the previous bitmap at the completion of the marking cycle.

Corresponding to the previous bitmap and the next bitmap, each G1 GC heap region has two top-at-mark-start (TAMS) fields respectively called previous TAMS (or PTAMS) and next TAMS (or NTAMS). The TAMS fields are useful in identifying objects allocated during a marking cycle.

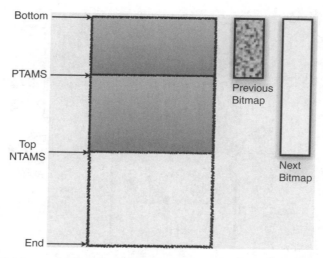

Figure 2.5 A heap region showing previous bitmap, next bitmap, PTAMS, and NTAMS during initial mark

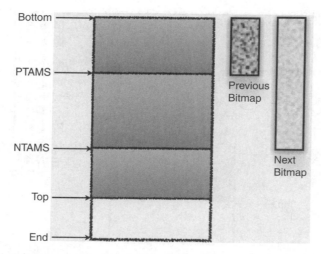

Figure 2.6 A heap region showing previous bitmap, next bitmap, PTAMS, and NTAMS during concurrent marking

At the start of a marking cycle, the NTAMS field is set to the current top of each region as shown in Figure 2.5. Objects that are allocated (or have died) since the start of the marking cycle are located above the corresponding TAMS value and are considered to be implicitly live. Live objects below TAMS need to be explicitly marked. Let's walk through an example: In Figure 2.6, we see a heap region during

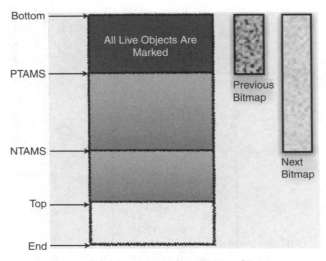

Figure 2.7 Step 1 with previous bitmap

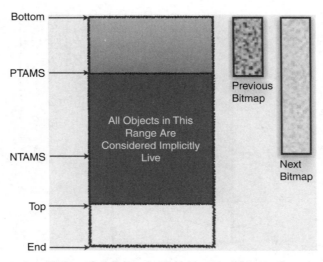

Figure 2.8 Step 2 with previous bitmap

concurrent marking, with "Previous Bitmap," "Next Bitmap," "PTAMS," "NTAMS," and "Top" as indicated. Live objects between PTAMS and the bottom (indicated as "Bottom" in the figures) of the heap are all marked and held in the previous bitmap as indicated in Figure 2.7. All objects between PTAMS and the top of the heap region are implicitly live (with respect to the previous bitmap) as shown in Figure 2.8. These

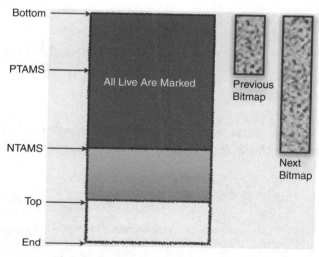

Figure 2.9 Step 1 with next bitmap

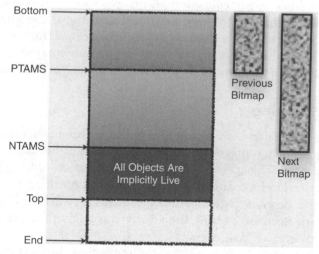

Figure 2.10 Step 2 with next bitmap

include the objects allocated during the concurrent marking and are thus allocated above the NTAMS and are implicitly live with respect to the next bitmap, as shown in Figure 2.10. At the end of the remark pause, all live objects above the PTAMS and below the NTAMS are completely marked as shown in Figure 2.9. As mentioned earlier, objects allocated during the concurrent marking cycle will be allocated above the NTAMS and are considered implicitly live with respect to the next bitmap (see Figure 2.10).

Stages of Concurrent Marking

The marking task chunks are carried out mostly concurrently. A few tasks are completed during short stop-the-world pauses. Let's now talk about the significance of these tasks.

Initial Mark

During initial mark, the mutator threads are stopped in order to facilitate the marking of all the objects in the Java heap that are directly reachable by the roots (also called root objects).

> **Tip**
>
> Root objects are objects that are reachable from outside of the Java heap; native stack objects and JNI (Java Native Interface) local or global objects are some examples.

Since the mutator threads are stopped, the initial-mark stage is a stop-the-world phase. Also, since young collection also traces roots and is stop-the-world, it's convenient (and time efficient) to carry out initial marking at the same time as a regular young collection. This is also known as "piggybacking." During the initial-mark pause, the NTAMS value for each region is set to the current top of the region (see Figure 2.5). This is done iteratively until all the regions of the heap are processed.

Root Region Scanning

After setting the TAMS for each region, the mutator threads are restarted, and the G1 GC now works concurrently with the mutator threads. For the correctness of the marking algorithm, the objects copied to the survivor regions during the initial-mark young collection need to be scanned and considered as marking roots. G1 GC hence starts scanning the survivor regions. Any object that is referenced from the survivor regions is marked. Because of this, the survivor regions that are scanned in this manner are referred to as "root regions."

The root region scanning stage must complete before the next garbage collection pause since all objects that are referenced from the survivor regions need to be identified and marked before the entire heap can be scanned for live objects.

Concurrent Marking

The concurrent marking stage is concurrent and multithreaded. The command-line option to set the number of concurrent threads to be used is -XX:ConcGCThreads. By default, G1 GC sets the total number of threads to one-fourth of the parallel

GC threads (-XX:ParallelGCThreads). The parallel GC threads are calculated by the JVM at the start of the VM. The concurrent threads scan a region at a time and use the "finger" pointer optimization to claim that region. This "finger" pointer optimization is similar to CMS GC's "finger" optimization and can be studied in [2].

As mentioned in the "RSets and Their Importance" section, G1 GC also employs a pre-write barrier to perform actions required by the SATB concurrent marking algorithm. As an application mutates its object graph, objects that were reachable at the start of marking and were a part of the snapshot may be overwritten before they are discovered and traced by a marking thread. Hence the SATB marking guarantee requires that the modifying mutator thread log the previous value of the pointer that needs to be modified, in an SATB log queue/buffer. This is called the "concurrent marking/SATB pre-write barrier" since the barrier code is executed before the update. The pre-write barrier enables the recording of the previous value of the object reference field so that concurrent marking can mark through the object whose value is being overwritten.

The pseudo-code of the pre-write barrier for an assignment of the form $x.f := y$ is as follows:

```
if (marking_is_active) {
    pre_val := x.f;
    if (pre_val != NULL) {
        satb_enqueue(pre_val);
    }
}
```

The marking_is_active condition is a simple check of a thread-local flag that is set to true at the start of marking, during the initial-mark pause. Guarding the rest of the pre-barrier code with this check reduces the overhead of executing the remainder of the barrier code when marking is not active. Since the flag is thread-local and its value may be loaded multiple times, it is likely that any individual check will hit in cache, further reducing the overhead of the barrier.

The satb_enqueue() first tries to enqueue the previous value in a thread-local buffer, referred to as an SATB buffer. The initial size of an SATB buffer is 256 entries, and each application thread has an SATB buffer. If there is no room to place the pre_val in the SATB buffer, the JVM runtime is called; the thread's current SATB buffer is retired and placed onto a global list of filled SATB buffers, a new SATB buffer is allocated for the thread, and the pre_val is recorded. It is the job of the concurrent marking threads to check and process the filled buffers at regular intervals to enable the marking of the logged objects.

The filled SATB buffers are processed (during the marking stage) from the global list by iterating through each buffer and marking each recorded object by setting the corresponding bit in the marking bitmap (and pushing the object onto a local marking stack if the object lies behind the finger). Marking then iterates over the set bits in a section of the marking bitmap, tracing the field references of the marked objects, setting more bits in the marking bitmap, and pushing objects as necessary.

Live data accounting is piggybacked on the marking operation. Hence, every time an object is marked, it is also counted (i.e., its bytes are added to the region's total). Only objects below NTAMS are marked and counted. At the end of this stage, the next marking bitmap is cleared so that it is ready when the next marking cycle starts. This is done concurrently with the mutator threads.

> **Tip**
>
> JDK 8u40 introduces a new command-line option `-XX:+ClassUnloading WithConcurrentMark` which, by default, enables class unloading with concurrent marking. Hence, concurrent marking can track classes and calculate their liveness. And during the remark stage, the unreachable classes can be unloaded.

Remark

The remark stage is the final marking stage. During this stop-the-world stage, G1 GC completely drains any remaining SATB log buffers and processes any updates. G1 GC also traverses any unvisited live objects. As of JDK 8u40, the remark stage is stop-the-world, since mutator threads are responsible for updating the SATB log buffers and as such "own" those buffers. Hence, a final stop-the-world pause is necessary to cover all the live data and safely complete live data accounting. In order to reduce time spent in this pause, multiple GC threads are used to parallel process the log buffers. The `-XX:ParallelGCThreads` help set the number of GC threads available during any GC pause. Reference processing is also a part of the remark stage.

> **Tip**
>
> Any application that heavily uses reference objects (weak references, soft references, phantom references, or final references) may see high remark times as a result of the reference-processing overhead. We will learn more about this in Chapter 3.

Cleanup

During the cleanup pause, the two marking bitmaps swap roles: the next marking bitmap becomes the previous one (given that the current marking cycle has been finalized and the next marking bitmap now has consistent marking information), and the previous marking bitmap becomes the next one (which will be used as the current marking bitmap during the next cycle). Similarly, PTAMS and NTAMS swap roles as well. Three major contributions of the cleanup pause are identifying completely free regions, sorting the heap regions to identify efficient old regions for mixed garbage collection, and RSet scrubbing. Current heuristics rank the regions according to liveness (the regions that have a lot of live objects are really expensive to collect, since copying is an expensive operation) and remembered set size (again, regions with large remembered sets are expensive to collect due to the regions' popularity—the concept of popularity was discussed in the "RSets and Their Importance" section). The goal is to collect/evacuate the candidate regions that are deemed less expensive (fewer live objects and less popular) first.

An advantage of identifying the live objects in each region is that on encountering a completely free region (that is, a region with no live objects), its remembered set can be cleared and the region can be immediately reclaimed and returned to the list of free regions instead of being placed in the GC-efficient (the concept of GC efficiency was discussed in the "Garbage Collection in G1" section) sorted array and having to wait for a reclamation (mixed) garbage collection pause. RSet scrubbing also helps detect stale references. So, for example, if marking finds that all the objects on a particular card are dead, the entry for that particular card is purged from the "owning" RSet.

Evacuation Failures and Full Collection

Sometimes G1 GC is unable to find a free region when trying to copy live objects from a young region or when trying to copy live objects during evacuation from an old region. Such a failure is reported as a to-space exhausted failure in the GC logs, and the duration of the failure is shown further down in the log as the Evacuation Failure time (331.5ms in the following example):

```
111.912: [GC pause (G1 Evacuation Pause) (young) (to-space exhausted),
0.6773162 secs]
<snip>
[Evacuation Failure: 331.5 ms]
```

There are other times when a humongous allocation may not be able to find contiguous regions in the old generation for allocating humongous objects.

At such times, the G1 GC will attempt to increase its usage of the Java heap. If the expansion of the Java heap space is unsuccessful, G1 GC triggers its fail-safe mechanism and falls back to a serial (single-threaded) full collection.

During a full collection, a single thread operates over the entire heap and does mark, sweep, and compaction of all the regions (expensive or otherwise) constituting the generations. After completion of the collection, the resultant heap now consists of purely live objects, and all the generations have been fully compacted.

> **Tip**
> Prior to JDK 8u40, unloading of classes was possible only at a full collection.

The single-threaded nature of the serial full collection and the fact that the collection spans the entire heap can make this a very expensive collection, especially if the heap size is fairly large. Hence, it is highly recommended that a nontrivial tuning exercise be done in such cases where full collections are a frequent occurrence.

> **Tip**
> For more information on how to get rid of evacuation failures, please refer to Chapter 3.

References

[1] Charlie Hunt and Binu John. *Java™ Performance*. Addison-Wesley, Upper Saddle River, NJ, 2012. ISBN 978-0-13-714252-1.

[2] Tony Printezis and David Detlefs. "A Generational Mostly-Concurrent Garbage Collector." *Proceedings of the 2nd International Symposium on Memory Management*. ACM, New York, 2000, pp. 143–54. ISBN 1-58113-263-8.

[3] Urs Hölzle. "A Fast Write Barrier for Generational Garbage Collectors." Presented at the OOPSLA'93 Garbage Collection Workshop, Washington, DC, October 1993.

[4] Darko Stefanovic, Matthew Hertz, Stephen M. Blackburn, Kathryn S McKinley, and J. Eliot B. Moss. "Older-First Garbage Collection in Practice: Evaluation in a Java Virtual Machine." *Proceedings of the 2002 Workshop on Memory System Performance*. ACM, New York, 2002, pp. 25–36.

[5] Taiichi Yuasa. "Real-Time Garbage Collection on General Purpose Machines." *Journal of Systems and Software,* Volume 11, Issue 3, March 1990, pp. 181–98. Elsevier Science, Inc., New York.

3

Garbage First Garbage Collector Performance Tuning

Performance engineering deals with the nonfunctional performance requirements of a system or its software and ensures that the design requirements are met in the product implementation. Thus it goes hand-in-hand with systems or software engineering.

In this chapter, we will discuss performance tuning in detail, concentrating on the newest garbage collector in Java HotSpot VM: Garbage First, or G1. We will skip young generation tuning advice already provided in *Java™ Performance* [1], particularly Chapter 7, "Tuning the JVM, Step by Step." Readers are encouraged to read that chapter and also the previous chapters in this supplemental book.

The Stages of a Young Collection

A G1 young collection has serial and parallel phases. The pause is serial in the sense that several tasks can be carried out only after certain other tasks are completed during a given stop-the-world pause. The parallel phases employ multiple GC worker threads that have their own work queues and can perform work stealing from other threads' work queues when their own queue tasks are completed.

> **Tip**
>
> The serial stages of the young collection pause can be multithreaded and use the value of `-XX:ParallelGCThreads` to determine the GC worker thread count.

Let's look at an excerpt from a G1 GC output log generated while running DaCapo with the HotSpot VM command-line option -XX:+PrintGCDetails. Here is the command-line and "Java version" output:

```
JAVA_OPTS="-XX:+UseG1GC -XX:+PrintGCDetails -Xloggc:jdk8u45_h2.log"
     MB:DaCapo mb$ java -version
     java version "1.8.0_45"
     Java(TM) SE Runtime Environment (build 1.8.0_45-b14)
     Java HotSpot(TM) 64-Bit Server VM (build 25.45-b02, mixed mode)
```

This is the GC log snippet (jdk8u45_h2.log):

```
108.815: [GC pause (G1 Evacuation Pause) (young), 0.0543862 secs]
   [Parallel Time: 52.1 ms, GC Workers: 8]
      [GC Worker Start (ms): Min: 108815.5, Avg: 108815.5, Max: 108815.6,
Diff: 0.1]
      [Ext Root Scanning (ms): Min: 0.1, Avg: 0.2, Max: 0.2, Diff: 0.1,
Sum: 1.2]
      [Update RS (ms): Min: 12.8, Avg: 13.0, Max: 13.2, Diff: 0.4, Sum:
103.6]
         [Processed Buffers: Min: 15, Avg: 16.0, Max: 17, Diff: 2, Sum: 128]
      [Scan RS (ms): Min: 13.4, Avg: 13.6, Max: 13.7, Diff: 0.3, Sum: 109.0]
      [Code Root Scanning (ms): Min: 0.0, Avg: 0.0, Max: 0.0, Diff: 0.0,
Sum: 0.1]
      [Object Copy (ms): Min: 25.1, Avg: 25.2, Max: 25.2, Diff: 0.1, Sum:
201.5]
      [Termination (ms): Min: 0.0, Avg: 0.0, Max: 0.0, Diff: 0.0, Sum: 0.1]
      [GC Worker Other (ms): Min: 0.0, Avg: 0.1, Max: 0.1, Diff: 0.1, Sum:
0.4]
      [GC Worker Total (ms): Min: 51.9, Avg: 52.0, Max: 52.1, Diff: 0.1,
Sum: 416.0]
      [GC Worker End (ms): Min: 108867.5, Avg: 108867.5, Max: 108867.6,
Diff: 0.1]
   [Code Root Fixup: 0.1 ms]
   [Code Root Purge: 0.0 ms]
   [Clear CT: 0.2 ms]
   [Other: 2.0 ms]
      [Choose CSet: 0.0 ms]
      [Ref Proc: 0.1 ms]
      [Ref Enq: 0.0 ms]
      [Redirty Cards: 0.2 ms]
      [Humongous Reclaim: 0.0 ms]
      [Free CSet: 1.2 ms]
   [Eden: 537.0M(537.0M)->0.0B(538.0M) Survivors: 23.0M->31.0M Heap:
849.2M(1024.0M)->321.4M(1024.0M)]
```

The snippet shows one G1 GC young collection pause, identified in the first line by (G1 Evacuation Pause) and (young). The line's timestamp is 108.815, and total pause time is 0.0543862 seconds:

```
108.815: [GC pause (G1 Evacuation Pause) (young), 0.0543862 secs]
```

Start of All Parallel Activities

The second line of the log snippet shows the total time spent in the parallel phase and the GC worker thread count:

```
[Parallel Time: 52.1 ms, GC Workers: 8]
```

The following lines show the major parallel work carried out by the eight worker threads:

```
[GC Worker Start (ms): Min: 108815.5, Avg: 108815.5, Max: 108815.6, Diff:
0.1]
[Ext Root Scanning (ms): Min: 0.1, Avg: 0.2, Max: 0.2, Diff: 0.1, Sum: 1.2]
[Update RS (ms): Min: 12.8, Avg: 13.0, Max: 13.2, Diff: 0.4, Sum: 103.6]
    [Processed Buffers: Min: 15, Avg: 16.0, Max: 17, Diff: 2, Sum: 128]
[Scan RS (ms): Min: 13.4, Avg: 13.6, Max: 13.7, Diff: 0.3, Sum: 109.0]
[Code Root Scanning (ms): Min: 0.0, Avg: 0.0, Max: 0.0, Diff: 0.0, Sum: 0.1]
[Object Copy (ms): Min: 25.1, Avg: 25.2, Max: 25.2, Diff: 0.1, Sum: 201.5]
[Termination (ms): Min: 0.0, Avg: 0.0, Max: 0.0, Diff: 0.0, Sum: 0.1]
[GC Worker Other (ms): Min: 0.0, Avg: 0.1, Max: 0.1, Diff: 0.1, Sum: 0.4]
[GC Worker Total (ms): Min: 51.9, Avg: 52.0, Max: 52.1, Diff: 0.1,
Sum: 416.0]
[GC Worker End (ms): Min: 108867.5, Avg: 108867.5, Max: 108867.6, Diff: 0.1]
```

GC Worker Start and GC Worker End tag the starting and ending timestamps respectively of the parallel phase. The Min timestamp for GC Worker Start is the time at which the first worker thread started; similarly, the Max timestamp for GC Worker End is the time at which the last worker thread completed all its tasks. The lines also contain Avg and Diff values in milliseconds. The things to look out for in those lines are:

- How far away the Diff value is from 0, 0 being the ideal.
- Any major variance in Max, Min, or Avg. This indicates that the worker threads could not start or finish their parallel work around the same time. That could mean that some sort of queue-handling issue exists that requires further analysis by looking at the parallel work done during the parallel phase.

External Root Regions

External root region scanning (`Ext Root Scanning`) is one of the first parallel tasks. During this phase the external (off-heap) roots such as the JVM's system dictionary, VM data structures, JNI thread handles, hardware registers, global variables, and thread stack roots are scanned to find out if any point into the current pause's collection set (CSet).

```
[Ext Root Scanning (ms): Min: 0.1, Avg: 0.2, Max: 0.2, Diff: 0.1, Sum: 1.2]
```

Here again, we look for `Diff >> 0` and major variance in `Max`, `Min`, or `Avg`.

> **Tip**
>
> The variance (`Diff`) is shown for all the timed activities that make up the parallel phase. A high variance usually means that the work is not balanced across the parallel threads for that particular activity. This knowledge is an analysis starting point, and ideally a deeper dive will identify the potential cause, which may require refactoring the Java application.

Another thing to watch out for is whether a worker thread is caught up in dealing with a single root. We have seen issues where the system dictionary, which is treated as a single root, ends up holding up a worker thread when there is a large number of loaded classes. When a worker thread is late for "termination" (explained later in this section), it is also considered held up.

Remembered Sets and Processed Buffers

```
[Update RS (ms): Min: 12.8, Avg: 13.0, Max: 13.2, Diff: 0.4, Sum: 103.6]
    [Processed Buffers: Min: 15, Avg: 16.0, Max: 17, Diff: 2, Sum: 128]
```

As explained in Chapter 2, "Garbage First Garbage Collection in Depth," G1 GC uses remembered sets (RSets) to help maintain and track references into G1 GC regions that "own" those RSets. The concurrent refinement threads, also discussed in Chapter 2, are tasked with scanning the update log buffers and updating RSets for the regions with dirty cards. In order to supplement the work carried out by the concurrent refinement threads, any remainder buffers that were logged but not yet processed by the refinement threads are handled during the parallel phase of the collection pause and are processed by the worker threads. These buffers are what are referred to as `Processed Buffers` in the log snippet.

In order to limit the time spent updating RSets, G1 sets a target time as a percentage of the pause time goal (-XX:MaxGCPauseMillis). The target time defaults to 10 percent of the pause time goal. Any evacuation pause should spend most of its time copying live objects, and 10 percent of the pause time goal is considered a reasonable amount of time to spend updating RSets. If after looking at the logs you realize that spending 10 percent of your pause time goal in updating RSets is undesirable, you can change the percentage by updating the -XX:G1RSetUpdatingPauseTime Percent command-line option to reflect your desired value. It is important to remember, however, that if the number of updated log buffers does not change, any decrease in RSet update time during the collection pause will result in fewer buffers being processed during that pause. This will push the log buffer update work off onto the concurrent refinement threads and will result in increased concurrent work and sharing of resources with the Java application mutator threads. Also, worst case, if the concurrent refinement threads cannot keep up with the log buffer update rate, the Java application mutators must step in and help with the processing—a scenario best avoided!

> **Tip**
>
> As discussed in Chapter 2, there is a command-line option called –XX:G1Conc RefinementThreads. By default it is set to the same value as –XX:ParallelGCThreads, which means that any change in XX:ParallelGCThreads will change the –XX:G1ConcRefinementThreads value as well.

Before collecting regions in the current CSet, the RSets for the regions in the CSet must be scanned for references into the CSet regions. As discussed in Chapter 2, a popular object in a region or a popular region itself can lead to its RSet being coarsened from a sparse PRT (per-region table) to a fine-grained PRT or even a coarsened bitmap, and thus scanning such an RSet will require more time. In such a scenario, you will see an increase in the Scan RS time shown here since the scan times depend on the coarseness gradient of the RSet data structures:

```
[Scan RS (ms): Min: 13.4, Avg: 13.6, Max: 13.7, Diff: 0.3, Sum: 109.0]
```

Another parallel task related to RSets is code root scanning, during which the code root set is scanned to find references into the current CSet:

```
[Code Root Scanning (ms): Min: 0.0, Avg: 0.0, Max: 0.0, Diff: 0.0543862,
Sum: 0.1]
```

In earlier versions of HotSpot, the entire code cache was treated as a single root and was claimed and processed by a single worker thread. A large and full or nearly full code cache would thus hold up that worker thread and lead to an increase in the total pause time. With the introduction of code root scanning as a separate parallel activity, the work of scanning the nmethods is reduced to just scanning the RSets for references from the compiled code. Hence for a particular region in the CSet, only if the RSet for that region has strong code roots is the corresponding nmethod scanned.

Tip

Developers often refer to the dynamically compiled code for a Java method by the HotSpot term of art *nmethod*. An nmethod is not to be confused with a native method, which refers to a JNI method. Nmethods include auxiliary information such as constant pools in addition to generated code.

Tip

To reduce nmethod scanning times, only the RSets of the regions in the CSet are scanned for references introduced by the compiler, rather than the "usual" references that are introduced by the Java application mutator threads.

Summarizing Remembered Sets

The option `-XX:+G1SummarizeRSetStats` can be used to provide a window into the total number of RSet coarsenings (fine-grained PRT or coarsened bitmap) to help determine if concurrent refinement threads are able to handle the updated buffers and to gather more information on nmethods. This option summarizes RSet statistics every nth GC pause, where n is set by `-XX:G1SummarizeRSetStatsPeriod=n`.

Tip

`-XX:+G1SummarizeRSetStats` is a diagnostic option and hence must be enabled by adding `-XX:+UnlockDiagnosticVMOptions` to the command line, for example,

```
JAVA_OPTS="-XX:+UseG1GC  -XX:+UnlockDiagnosticVMOptions  -XX:
+PrintGCDetails  -XX:+G1SummarizeRSetStats  -XX:G1Summarize
RSetStatsPeriod=1 -Xloggc:jdk8u45_h2.log".
```

Here is a GC log snippet with the RSets summarized on every GC pause:

```
Before GC RS summary

 Recent concurrent refinement statistics
  Processed 23270 cards
  Of 96 completed buffers:
         96 (100.0%) by concurrent RS threads.
          0 (  0.0%) by mutator threads.
  Did 0 coarsenings.
  Concurrent RS threads times (s)
         1.29      1.29      1.29      1.29     1.29     1.29     1.29     0.00
  Concurrent sampling threads times (s)
         0.97

 Current rem set statistics
  Total per region rem sets sizes = 4380K. Max = 72K.
        767K ( 17.5%) by 212 Young regions
         29K (  0.7%) by 9 Humongous regions
       2151K ( 49.1%) by 648 Free regions
       1431K ( 32.7%) by 155 Old regions
   Static structures = 256K, free_lists = 0K.
    816957 occupied cards represented.
         13670 (  1.7%) entries by 212 Young regions
             4 (  0.0%) entries by 9 Humongous regions
             0 (  0.0%) entries by 648 Free regions
        803283 ( 98.3%) entries by 155 Old regions
   Region with largest rem set =
4:(O)[0x00000006c0400000,0x00000006c0500000,0x00000006c0500000],
size = 72K, occupied = 190K.
  Total heap region code root sets sizes = 40K.  Max = 22K.
         3K (  8.7%) by 212 Young regions
         0K (  0.3%) by 9 Humongous regions
        10K ( 24.8%) by 648 Free regions
        27K ( 66.2%) by 155 Old regions
    1035 code roots represented.
            5 (  0.5%) elements by 212 Young regions
            0 (  0.0%) elements by 9 Humongous regions
            0 (  0.0%) elements by 648 Free regions
         1030 ( 99.5%) elements by 155 Old regions
   Region with largest amount of code roots =
4:(O)[0x00000006c0400000,0x00000006c0500000,0x00000006c0500000],
size = 22K, num_elems = 0.
```

```
After GC RS summary

 Recent concurrent refinement statistics
  Processed 3782 cards
  Of 26 completed buffers:
         26 (100.0%) by concurrent RS threads.
          0 (  0.0%) by mutator threads.
  Did 0 coarsenings.
  Concurrent RS threads times (s)
         0.00      0.00      0.00     0.00     0.00     0.00     0.00     0.00
```

Continued

```
Concurrent sampling threads times (s)
        0.00

Current rem set statistics
 Total per region rem sets sizes = 4329K. Max = 73K.
         33K (  0.8%) by 10 Young regions
         29K (  0.7%) by 9 Humongous regions
       2689K ( 62.1%) by 810 Free regions
       1577K ( 36.4%) by 195 Old regions
  Static structures = 256K, free_lists = 63K.
   805071 occupied cards represented.
          0 (  0.0%) entries by 10 Young regions
          4 (  0.0%) entries by 9 Humongous regions
          0 (  0.0%) entries by 810 Free regions
     805067 (100.0%) entries by 195 Old regions
   Region with largest rem set =
4:(O)[0x00000006c0400000,0x00000006c0500000,0x00000006c0500000],
size = 73K, occupied = 190K.
   Total heap region code root sets sizes = 40K.  Max = 22K.
         0K (  0.8%) by 10 Young regions
         0K (  0.3%) by 9 Humongous regions
        12K ( 30.9%) by 810 Free regions
        27K ( 68.0%) by 195 Old regions
     1036 code roots represented.
          2 (  0.2%) elements by 10 Young regions
          0 (  0.0%) elements by 9 Humongous regions
          0 (  0.0%) elements by 810 Free regions
       1034 ( 99.8%) elements by 195 Old regions
   Region with largest amount of code roots =
4:(O)[0x00000006c0400000,0x00000006c0500000,0x00000006c0500000],
size = 22K, num_elems = 0.
```

The main things to look out for in this snippet are as follows:

```
Processed 23270 cards
  Of 96 completed buffers:
         96 (100.0%) by concurrent RS threads.
          0 (  0.0%) by mutator threads.
and
Did 0 coarsenings.
```

The log output is printed for both before and after the GC pause. The `Processed cards` tag summarizes the work done by the concurrent refinement threads and sometimes, though very rarely, the Java application mutator threads. In this case, 96 completed buffers had 23,270 processed cards, and all (100 percent) of the work was done by the concurrent RSet refinement threads. There were no RSet coarsenings as indicated by `Did 0 coarsenings`.

Other parts of the log output describe concurrent RSet times and current RSet statistics, including their sizes and occupied cards per region type (young, free, humongous, or old). You can use the log to figure out how the code root sets are referencing the RSets for each region type as well as the total number of references per region type.

Tip

The ability to visualize four areas of potential improvement—RSet coarsenings, updating RSets, scanning RSets, and scanning nmethods referencing RSets—can help significantly in understanding your application and may pave the way for application improvements.

Evacuation and Reclamation

Now that G1 knows about its CSet for the current collection pause, along with a complete set of references into the CSet, it can move on to the most expensive part of a pause: the evacuation of live objects from the CSet regions and reclamation of the newly freed space. Ideally, the object copy times are the biggest contributor to the pause. Live objects that need to be evacuated are copied to thread-local GC allocation buffers (GCLABs) allocated in target regions. Worker threads compete to install a forwarding pointer to the newly allocated copy of the old object image. With the help of work stealing [2], a single "winner" thread helps with copying and scanning the object. Work stealing also provides load balancing between the worker threads.

```
[Object Copy (ms): Min: 25.1, Avg: 25.2, Max: 25.2, Diff: 0.1, Sum: 201.5]
```

Tip

G1 GC uses the copy times as weighted averages to predict the time it takes to copy a single region. Users can adjust the young generation size if the prediction logic fails to keep up with the desired pause time goal.

Termination

After completing the tasks just described, each worker thread offers termination if its work queue is empty. A thread requesting termination checks the other threads' work queues to attempt work stealing. If no work is available, it terminates. `Termination` tags the time that each worker thread spends in this termination protocol. A GC worker thread that gets caught up in a single root scan can be late to complete all the tasks in its queue and hence eventually be late for termination.

```
[Termination (ms): Min: 0.0, Avg: 0.0, Max: 0.0, Diff: 0.0, Sum: 0.1]
```

If any (or all) worker threads are getting caught up somewhere, it will show up in long termination times and may indicate a work-stealing or load-balancing issue.

Parallel Activity Outside of GC

Termination marks the end of parallel activities for worker threads during the evacuation/collection pause. The next line in the log snippet, tagged GC Worker Other, is time spent in the parallel phase but not in any of the "usual" parallel activities described so far. Though attributed to "GC time," it could very easily be occupied by something outside of the GC that happens to occur during the parallel phase of the GC pause. GC threads are stopped during this period. We have seen GC Worker Other times being high when there is an increase in compiler work due to JVM activities as a result of ill-considered compiler options. If you observe long times here, investigate such non-GC activities.

```
[GC Worker Other (ms): Min: 0.0, Avg: 0.1, Max: 0.1, Diff: 0.1, Sum: 0.4]
```

Summarizing All Parallel Activities

The last line of the parallel phase, tagged GC Worker Total, is the sum of the "usual" and "unusual" GC worker thread times:

```
[GC Worker Total (ms): Min: 51.9, Avg: 52.0, Max: 52.1, Diff: 0.1,
Sum: 416.0]
```

Start of All Serial Activities

After the parallel phase is complete, the serial phase begins with the lines tagged Code Root Fixup, Code Root Purge, and Clear CT. During these times, the main GC thread updates code roots with the new location of evacuated objects and also purges the code root set table. The Clear CT phase (which is carried out in parallel with the help of parallel worker threads) clears the card table marks, as mentioned in Chapter 2, when scanning RSets; once a card is scanned, G1 GC marks a corresponding entry in the global card table to avoid rescanning that card. This mark is cleared during the Clear CT phase of the pause.

Tip

The main GC thread is the VM thread that executes the GC VM operation during a safepoint.

```
[Code Root Fixup: 0.1 ms]
[Code Root Purge: 0.0 ms]
[Clear CT: 0.2 ms]
```

Tip

During a mixed collection pause, `Code Root Fixup` will include the time spent in updating non-evacuated regions.

Other Serial Activities

The final part of the sequential phase is tagged `Other`. The bigger contributors to `Other` involve choosing the CSet for the collection, reference processing and enqueuing, card redirtying, reclaiming free humongous regions, and freeing the CSet after the collection. These major contributors are shown the `PrintGCDetails` output:

```
[Other: 2.0 ms]
   [Choose CSet: 0.0 ms]
   [Ref Proc: 0.1 ms]
   [Ref Enq: 0.0 ms]
   [Redirty Cards: 0.2 ms]
   [Humongous Reclaim: 0.0 ms]
   [Free CSet: 1.2 ms]
```

Tip

For a young collection all the young regions are collected, hence there is no "choosing" as such since all the young regions automatically become a part of the young CSet. The "choosing" occurs for a mixed collection pausse and becomes an important factor in understanding how to "tame" your mixed collections. We will discuss choosing the CSet in detail later in this chapter.

Reference processing and enqueuing are for soft, weak, phantom, final, and JNI references. We discuss this and more in the section titled "Reference Processing Tuning."

The act of reference enqueuing may require updating the RSets. Hence, the updates need to be logged and their associated cards need to be marked as dirty.

The time spent redirtying the cards is shown as the `Redirty Cards` time (0.2 ms in the preceding example).

`Humongous Reclaim` is new in JDK 8u40. If a humongous object is found to be unreachable by looking at all references from the root set or young generation regions and by making sure that there are no references to the humongous object in the RSet, that object can be reclaimed during the evacuation pause. (See Chapter 2 for detailed descriptions of humongous regions and humongous objects.)

The remainder of the `Other` time is spent in fixing JNI handles and similar work. The collective time in `Other` should be very small, and any time hog should have a reasonable explanation. As an example, you could see higher times in `Free CSet` if your CSet per pause is very large. Similarly, `Ref Proc` and `Ref Enq` could show higher times depending on how many references are used in your application. Similar reasoning can be applied to `Humongous Reclaim` times, if you have many short-lived humongous objects.

Young Generation Tunables

As covered in *Java™ Performance* [1], Chapter 7, "Tuning the JVM, Step by Step," there are some tunables that can help with tuning the young generation itself.

G1 GC has great tuning potential. There are initial and default values that help G1 GC's heuristics, and in order to be able to tune G1 GC, one needs to understand these defaults and their effect on the heuristics. Options such as `-XX:MaxGCPauseMillis` (pause time goal; defaults to 200 ms), `-XX:G1NewSizePercent` (initial young generation size expressed as a percentage of the total heap; defaults to 5 percent), and `-XX:G1MaxNewSizePercent` (maximum young generation growth limit expressed as a percentage of the total heap; defaults to 60 percent) help grow or shrink the young generation based on the initial and upper bounds, the pause time goal, and the weighted average of previous copy times. If there is a good understanding of the workload and if there is a perceived benefit from circumventing the adaptive resizing (for example, if you see that the predicted time varies drastically from the actual time observed), you can adjust the defaults. The side effect is that you are forgoing adaptive resizing for more predictable limits. Another thing to keep in mind is that the new limits are applicable only to the one application that you are tuning and will not carry forward to any other/different applications that may have similar pause time requirements since most applications exhibit different behaviors based on their allocation rates, promotion rates, steady and transient live data sets, object sizes, and life spans.

Let's look at some examples. These are once again run using JDK 8u45 with different values for `-XX:MaxGCPauseMillis` (as can be seen in the time noted as the `target pause time`). The benchmark suite was DaCapo, and `-XX:+PrintAdaptiveSizePolicy` was enabled at the JVM command line.

```
  6.317: [GC pause (G1 Evacuation Pause) (young) 6.317: [G1Ergonomics (CSet
Construction) start choosing CSet, _pending_cards: 5800, predicted base
time: 20.39 ms, remaining time: 179.61 ms, target pause time: 200.00 ms]
  6.317: [G1Ergonomics (CSet Construction) add young regions to CSet, eden:
225 regions, survivors: 68 regions, predicted young region time: 202.05
ms]
  6.317: [G1Ergonomics (CSet Construction) finish choosing CSet, eden: 225
regions, survivors: 68 regions, old: 0 regions, predicted pause time:
222.44 ms, target pause time: 200.00 ms]
, 0.1126312 secs]
```

In the above example, the pause time goal was left at its default value of 200ms, and it was observed that even though the prediction logic predicted the pause time to be 222.44ms, the actual pause time was only 112.63 ms. In this case, we could have easily added more young regions to the CSet.

```
36.931: [GC pause (G1 Evacuation Pause) (young) 36.931: [G1Ergonomics
(CSet Construction) start choosing CSet, _pending_cards: 9129, predicted
base time: 14.46 ms, remaining time: 35.54 ms, target pause time: 50.00
ms]
 36.931: [G1Ergonomics (CSet Construction) add young regions to CSet,
eden: 284 regions, survivors: 16 regions, predicted young region time:
60.90 ms]
 36.931: [G1Ergonomics (CSet Construction) finish choosing CSet, eden:
284 regions, survivors: 16 regions, old: 0 regions, predicted pause time:
75.36 ms, target pause time: 50.00 ms]
, 0.0218629 secs]
```

The second example above showcases a similar scenario to the one shown before, only here the pause time target was changed to 50 ms (no adjustments were made to the young generation). Once again, the prediction logic was off and it predicted a pause time of 75.36 ms, whereas the actual pause time was 21.86 ms.

After adjusting the young generation (as can be seen in the number of eden and survivor regions added to the CSet in the third example, below), we could get the pause times to be in the 50 ms range as shown here:

```
58.373: [GC pause (G1 Evacuation Pause) (young) 58.373: [G1Ergonomics
(CSet Construction) start choosing CSet, _pending_cards: 5518, predicted
base time: 10.00 ms, remaining time: 40.00 ms, target pause time: 50.00
ms]
 58.373: [G1Ergonomics (CSet Construction) add young regions to CSet,
eden: 475 regions, survivors: 25 regions, predicted young region time:
168.35 ms]
 58.373: [G1Ergonomics (CSet Construction) finish choosing CSet, eden:
475 regions, survivors: 25 regions, old: 0 regions, predicted pause time:
178.35 ms, target pause time: 50.00 ms]
, 0.0507471 secs]
```

Here, even though the prediction logic is still way off, our pause time (50.75 ms) is in the desired range (50 ms).

Concurrent Marking Phase Tunables

For G1, the tunable `-XX:InitiatingHeapOccupancyPercent=n` (here n defaults to 45 percent of the total Java heap size and takes into account the old generation occupancy, which include old and humongous regions) helps with deciding when to initiate the concurrent marking cycle.

> **Tip**
>
> Unlike CMS GC's initiation of a marking cycle, which is with respect to its old generation size, G1's `InitiatingHeapOccupancyPercent` is with respect to the entire Java heap size.

The concurrent marking cycle starts with an initial marking pause which happens at the same time as (aka, is "piggybacked onto") a young collection pause. This pause marks the beginning of the collection cycle and is followed by other concurrent and parallel tasks for root region scanning, concurrent marking and liveness accounting, final mark, and cleanup. Figure 3.1 shows all the pauses in a concurrent marking cycle: initial mark, remark, and cleanup. To learn more about the concurrent marking cycle please refer to Chapter 2.

```
277.559: [GC pause (G1 Evacuation Pause) (young) (initial-mark), 0.0960289
secs]
```

The concurrent marking tasks can take a long time if the application's live object graph is large and may often be interrupted by young collection pauses. The concurrent marking cycle must be complete before a mixed collection pause can start and is immediately followed by a young collection that calculates the thresholds required to trigger a mixed collection on the next pause, as shown in Figure 3.1. The figure shows an initial-mark pause (which, as mentioned earlier, piggybacks on a young collection). There could be more than one young collection when the concurrent phase is under way (only one pause is shown in the figure). The final mark (also known as remark) completes the marking, and a small cleanup pause helps with the cleanup activities as described in Chapter 2. There is a young generation evacuation pause right after the cleanup pause which helps prepare for the mixed collection cycle. The four pauses after this young collection pause are the mixed collection evacuation pauses that successfully collect all the garbage out of the target CSet regions.

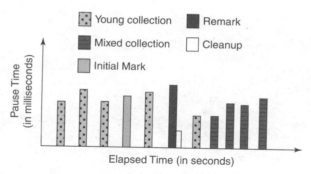

Figure 3.1 Young collection pauses, mixed collection pauses, and pauses in a concurrent marking cycle

If any of the concurrent marking tasks and hence the entire cycle take too long to complete, a mixed collection pause is delayed, which could eventually lead to an evacuation failure. An evacuation failure will show up as a `to-space exhausted` message on the GC log, and the total time attributed to the failure will be shown in the `Other` section of the pause. Here is an example log snippet:

```
276.731: [GC pause (G1 Evacuation Pause) (young) (to-space exhausted),
0.8272932 secs]
    [Parallel Time: 387.0 ms, GC Workers: 8]
        [GC Worker Start (ms): Min: 276731.9, Avg: 276731.9, Max: 276732.1,
Diff: 0.2]
        [Ext Root Scanning (ms): Min: 0.0, Avg: 0.2, Max: 0.2, Diff: 0.2,
Sum: 1.3]
        [Update RS (ms): Min: 17.0, Avg: 17.2, Max: 17.3, Diff: 0.4, Sum:
137.3]
            [Processed Buffers: Min: 19, Avg: 21.0, Max: 23, Diff: 4, Sum: 168]
        [Scan RS (ms): Min: 10.5, Avg: 10.7, Max: 10.9, Diff: 0.4, Sum: 85.4]
        [Code Root Scanning (ms): Min: 0.0, Avg: 0.0, Max: 0.0, Diff: 0.0,
Sum: 0.1]
        [Object Copy (ms): Min: 358.7, Avg: 358.8, Max: 358.9, Diff: 0.2,
Sum: 2870.3]
        [Termination (ms): Min: 0.0, Avg: 0.1, Max: 0.1, Diff: 0.1, Sum: 0.7]
        [GC Worker Other (ms): Min: 0.0, Avg: 0.0, Max: 0.0, Diff: 0.0, Sum:
0.2]
        [GC Worker Total (ms): Min: 386.7, Avg: 386.9, Max: 387.0, Diff:
0.2, Sum: 3095.3]
        [GC Worker End (ms): Min: 277118.8, Avg: 277118.8, Max: 277118.9,
Diff: 0.0]
    [Code Root Fixup: 0.1 ms]
    [Code Root Purge: 0.0 ms]
    [Clear CT: 0.2 ms]
```

Continued

```
[Other: 440.0 ms]
    [Evacuation Failure: 437.5 ms]
    [Choose CSet: 0.0 ms]
    [Ref Proc: 0.1 ms]
    [Ref Enq: 0.0 ms]
    [Redirty Cards: 0.9 ms]
    [Humongous Reclaim: 0.0 ms]
    [Free CSet: 0.9 ms]
  [Eden: 831.0M(900.0M)->0.0B(900.0M) Survivors: 0.0B->0.0B Heap:
1020.1M(1024.0M)->1020.1M(1024.0M)]
 [Times: user=3.64 sys=0.20, real=0.83 secs]
```

When you see such messages in your log, you can try the following to avoid the problem:

- It is imperative to set the marking threshold to fit your application's static plus transient live data needs. If you set the marking threshold too high, you risk running into evacuation failures. If you set the marking threshold too low, you may prematurely trigger concurrent cycles and may reclaim close to no space during your mixed collections. It is generally better to err on the side of starting the marking cycle too early rather than too late, since the negative consequences of an evacuation failure tend to be greater than those of the marking cycle running too frequently.

- If you think that the marking threshold is correct, but the concurrent cycle is still taking too long and your mixed collections end up "losing the race" to reclaim regions and triggering evacuation failures, try increasing your total concurrent thread count. -XX:ConcGCThreads defaults to one-fourth of -XX:Parallel GCThreads. You can either increase the concurrent thread count directly or increase the parallel GC thread count, which effectively increases the concurrent thread count.

Tip

Increasing the concurrent thread count will take processing time away from mutator (Java application) threads since the concurrent GC threads work at the same time as your application threads.

A Refresher on the Mixed Garbage Collection Phase

Now that we have tuned young collections and concurrent marking cycles, we can focus on old generation collection carried out by mixed collection cycles. Recall from Chapter 2 that a mixed collection CSet consists of all the young regions plus a few regions selected from the old generation. Tuning mixed collections can be broken down to varying the number of old regions in the mixed collection's CSet and adding enough back-to-back mixed collections to diffuse the cost of any single one of them over the time it takes to collect all eligible old regions. Taming mixed collections will help you achieve your system-level agreement for GC overhead and responsiveness.

The -XX:+PrintAdaptiveSizePolicy option dumps details of G1's ergonomics heuristic decisions. An example follows.

First the command line:

```
JAVA_OPTS="-XX:+UseG1GC -XX:+PrintGCDetails -XX:+PrintAdaptiveSizePolicy
-Xloggc:jdk8u45_h2.log"
```

And the log snippet:

```
97.859: [GC pause (G1 Evacuation Pause) (mixed) 97.859: [G1Ergonomics
(CSet Construction) start choosing CSet, _pending_cards: 28330, predicted
base time: 17.45 ms, remaining time: 182.55 ms, target pause time: 200.00
ms]
 97.859: [G1Ergonomics (CSet Construction) add young regions to CSet,
eden: 37 regions, survivors: 14 regions, predicted young region time:
16.12 ms]
 97.859: [G1Ergonomics (CSet Construction) finish adding old regions to
CSet, reason: old CSet region num reached max, old: 103 regions, max: 103
regions]
 97.859: [G1Ergonomics (CSet Construction) finish choosing CSet, eden: 37
regions, survivors: 14 regions, old: 103 regions, predicted pause time:
123.38 ms, target pause time: 200.00 ms]
 97.905: [G1Ergonomics (Mixed GCs) continue mixed GCs, reason: candidate
old regions available, candidate old regions: 160 regions, reclaimable:
66336328 bytes (6.18 %), threshold: 5.00 %]
, 0.0467862 secs]
```

The first line tells us the evacuation pause type, in this case a mixed collection, and the predicted times for activities such as CSet selection and adding young and old regions to the CSet.

On the fifth timestamp, tagged Mixed GCs, you can see G1 decide to continue with mixed collections since there are candidate regions available and reclaimable bytes are still higher than the default 5 percent threshold.

This example highlights two tunables: the number of old regions to be added to the CSet as can be seen here:

```
97.859: [G1Ergonomics (CSet Construction) finish adding old regions
to CSet, reason: old CSet region num reached max, old: 103 regions,
max: 103 regions]
```

and the reclaimable percentage threshold:

```
97.905: [G1Ergonomics (Mixed GCs) continue mixed GCs, reason: candidate
old regions available, candidate old regions: 160 regions, reclaimable:
66336328 bytes (6.18 %), threshold: 5.00 %]
```

Let's talk more about these and other tunables next.

The Taming of a Mixed Garbage Collection Phase

The reclaimable percentage threshold, -XX:G1HeapWastePercent, is a measure of the total amount of garbage (or fragmentation, if you prefer) that you are able to tolerate in your application. It is expressed as a percentage of the application's total Java heap and defaults to 5 percent (JDK 8u45). Let's look at an example:

```
123.563: [GC pause (G1 Evacuation Pause) (mixed) 123.563: [G1Ergonomics
(CSet Construction) start choosing CSet, _pending_cards: 7404, predicted
base time: 6.13 ms, remaining time: 43.87 ms, target pause time: 50.00 ms]
  123.563: [G1Ergonomics (CSet Construction) add young regions to CSet,
eden: 464 regions, survivors: 36 regions, predicted young region time:
80.18 ms]
  123.563: [G1Ergonomics (CSet Construction) finish adding old regions
to CSet, reason: predicted time is too high, predicted time: 0.70 ms,
remaining time: 0.00 ms, old: 24 regions, min: 24 regions]
  123.563: [G1Ergonomics (CSet Construction) added expensive regions to
CSet, reason: old CSet region num not reached min, old: 24 regions,
expensive: 24 regions, min: 24 regions, remaining time: 0.00 ms]
  123.563: [G1Ergonomics (CSet Construction) finish choosing CSet, eden:
464 regions, survivors: 36 regions, old: 24 regions, predicted pause time:
101.83 ms, target pause time: 50.00 ms]
  123.640: [G1Ergonomics (Mixed GCs) continue mixed GCs, reason: candidate
old regions available, candidate old regions: 165 regions, reclaimable:
109942200 bytes (10.24 %), threshold: 5.00 %]
, 0.0771597 secs]
```

The last line of this example shows that mixed GCs will be continued since there is enough garbage to be reclaimed (10.24 percent). Here the reclaimable percentage threshold is kept at its default value of 5 percent.

If mixed collections are becoming exponentially expensive as can be seen in Figure 3.2, increasing this threshold will help. Remember, however, that the increase will leave more regions fragmented and occupied. This means that the old generation will retain more (transient) live data, which must be accounted for by adjusting your marking threshold accordingly.

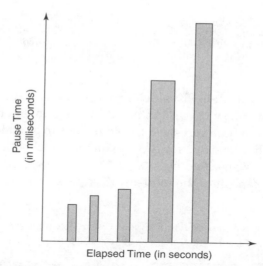

Figure 3.2 Mixed GC collection cycle showing exponentially expensive collection times

The minimum threshold for the number of old regions to be included in the CSet per mixed collection pause within a mixed collection cycle is specified by -XX:G1MixedGCCountTarget and defaults to 8. As briefly discussed in Chapter 2, the minimum number of old regions per mixed collection pause is

Minimum old CSet size per mixed collection pause = Total number of candidate old regions identified for mixed collection cycle/G1MixedGCCountTarget

This formula determines the minimum number of old regions per CSet for each mixed collection to be *x* such as to facilitate *y* back-to-back mixed collections that will collect all candidate old regions. The set of back-to-back mixed collections carried out after a completed concurrent marking cycle constitutes a mixed collection cycle. Let's look at line 4 of the preceding example:

```
123.563: [G1Ergonomics (CSet Construction) added expensive regions to
CSet, reason: old CSet region num not reached min, old: 24 regions,
expensive: 24 regions, min: 24 regions, remaining time: 0.00 ms]
```

Line 4 tells us that only 24 regions were added to the CSet, since the minimum number of old regions to be added per CSet was not met. The previous (young) collection pause tells us that there are 189 candidate old regions available for reclamation, hence G1 GC should start a mixed collection cycle:

```
117.378: [G1Ergonomics (Mixed GCs) start mixed GCs, reason: candidate
old regions available, candidate old regions: 189 regions, reclaimable:
134888760 bytes (12.56 %), threshold: 5.00 %]
```

So, dividing 189 by the default value of `G1MixedGCCountTarget` (8) = Ceiling (189/8) = 24. And that is how we get to the minimum number of 24 regions.

Just as there is a minimum threshold for old regions to be added to the CSet, there is a maximum as well. The value for the maximum threshold for the old regions to be added to the CSet is specified by `-XX:G1OldCSetRegionThresholdPercent`, which defaults to 10 percent of the total Java heap size. Once again, let's look at an example:

```
97.859: [GC pause (G1 Evacuation Pause) (mixed) 97.859: [G1Ergonomics
(CSet Construction) start choosing CSet, _pending_cards: 28330, predicted
base time: 17.45 ms, remaining time: 182.55 ms, target pause time: 200.00
ms]
 97.859: [G1Ergonomics (CSet Construction) add young regions to CSet,
eden: 37 regions, survivors: 14 regions, predicted young region time:
16.12 ms]
 97.859: [G1Ergonomics (CSet Construction) finish adding old regions to
CSet, reason: old CSet region num reached max, old: 103 regions, max: 103
regions]
 97.859: [G1Ergonomics (CSet Construction) finish choosing CSet, eden: 37
regions, survivors: 14 regions, old: 103 regions, predicted pause time:
123.38 ms, target pause time: 200.00 ms]
 97.905: [G1Ergonomics (Mixed GCs) continue mixed GCs, reason: candidate
old regions available, candidate old regions: 160 regions, reclaimable:
66336328 bytes (6.18 %), threshold: 5.00 %]
```

Lines 3 and 5 show that even though there were more candidate old regions available for collection, the total number of old regions in the current CSet was capped at 103 regions. As mentioned in the preceding description, the 103 region count comes from the total heap size of 1G and the 10 percent default value for `G1OldCSetRegionThresholdPercent`, which rounds up to 103.

Now that we know how to specify the minimum and maximum number of regions per CSet per mixed collection, we can modify the thresholds to suit our pause time goal and at the same time maintain the desired amount of transient live data in the old generation.

The `-XX:G1MixedGCLiveThresholdPercent` option, which defaults to 85 percent (JDK 8u45), is the maximum percentage of live data within a region that will allow it to be included in a CSet. Per-region live data percentages are computed during the concurrent marking phase. An old region deemed to be too expensive to evacuate—that is, whose live data percentage is above the liveness threshold—is not included as a CSet candidate region. This option directly controls fragmentation per region, so be careful.

Tip

Increasing the `G1MixedGCLiveThresholdPercent` value means that it will take longer to evacuate old regions, which means that mixed collection pauses will also be longer.

Avoiding Evacuation Failures

In the "Concurrent Marking Phase Tunables" section, we discussed a couple of ways to avoid evacuation failures. Here are a few more important tuning parameters:

- Heap size. Make sure that you can accommodate all the static and transient live data and your short- and medium-lived application data in your Java heap. Apart from the accommodation of live data, additional Java heap space, or headroom, should be available in order for GC to operate efficiently. The more the available headroom, the higher the possible throughput and/or the lower the possible latency.

- Avoid over-specifying your JVM command-line options! Let the defaults work for you. Get a baseline with just your initial and maximum heap settings and a desired pause time goal. If you already know that the default marking threshold is not helping, add your tuned marking threshold on the command line for the baseline run. So, your base command would look something like this:

  ```
  -Xms2g -Xmx4g -XX:MaxGCPauseMillis=100
  ```
  or
  ```
  -Xms2g -Xmx4g -XX:MaxGCPauseMillis=100 -
  XX:InitiatingHeapOccupancyPercent=55
  ```

- If your application has long-lived humongous objects, make sure that your marking threshold is set low enough to accommodate them. Also, make sure that the long-lived objects that you deem "humongous" are treated as such by G1. You can ensure this by setting `-XX:G1HeapRegionSize` to a value that guarantees that objects greater than or equal to 50 percent of the region size are treated as humongous. As mentioned in Chapter 2, the default value is calculated based on your initial and maximum heap sizes and can range from 1 to 32MB.

  Here is a log snippet using `-XX:+PrintAdaptiveSizePolicy`:

```
  91.890: [G1Ergonomics (Concurrent Cycles) request concurrent cycle
initiation, reason: occupancy higher than threshold, occupancy: 483393536
bytes, allocation request: 2097168 bytes, threshold: 483183810 bytes
(45.00 %), source: concurrent humongous allocation]
```

A concurrent cycle is being requested since the heap occupancy crossed the marking threshold due to a humongous allocation request. The request was for 2,097,168 bytes, which is far larger than the 1MB G1 heap region size default set by G1 at JVM start-up time.

- There are times when evacuation failures are caused by not having enough space in the survivor regions for newly promoted objects. When you observe this happening, try increasing -XX:G1ReservePercent. The reserve percent creates a false ceiling for the reserved space so as to accommodate any variation in promotion patterns. The default value is 10 percent of the total Java heap and is limited by G1 to 50 percent of the total Java heap since more would amount to a very large amount of wasted reserve space.

Reference Processing

Garbage collection must treat Java reference objects—phantom references, soft references, and weak references—differently from other Java objects. Reference objects require more work to collect than non-reference objects.

In this section, you will learn how to identify if the time required to perform reference processing during a G1 garbage collection pause is an issue for your application and how to tune G1 to reduce this overhead, along with tips for isolating which reference object type is inducing the most overhead. Depending on the application and its pause time requirements, refactoring the application's source code may be required to reduce reference processing overhead.

> **Tip**
>
> Java Platform, Standard Edition (Java SE) API documentation for each of the reference object types (http://docs.oracle.com/javase/8/docs/api) and the java.lang.ref package APIs for phantom reference, soft reference, and weak reference are both good sources for understanding how each reference object type behaves and how and when they are garbage collected.

Observing Reference Processing

There are several major activities associated with garbage collecting reference objects: discovering the reference objects, pushing them onto the JVM's reference queue, and pulling them off the reference queue and processing them. When using G1 with -XX:+PrintGCDetails, the time spent enqueuing reference objects is reported separately from the time spent processing them. The two times are reported in the `Other` section of the log on both young and mixed GCs:

```
[Other: 9.9 ms]
    [Choose CSet: 0.0 ms]
    [Ref Proc: 8.2 ms]
    [Ref Enq: 0.3 ms]
    [Redirty Cards: 0.7 ms]
    [Humongous Reclaim: 0.0 ms]
    [Free CSet: 0.5 ms]
```

`Ref Proc` is the time spent processing reference objects, and `Ref Enq` is the time spent enqueuing reference objects. As the example suggests, the time spent in `Ref Enq` is rarely as long as the time spent in `Ref Proc`. In fact, we have yet to see an application that consistently has higher `Ref Enq` times. If it happens, it means that the amount of effort required to process a reference is very small relative to its enqueuing time, which is unlikely for most reference object types.

G1 also reports reference processing activity during the remark phase during G1's concurrent cycle. Using `-XX:+PrintGCDetails`, the log output from remark will include reference processing time:

```
[GC remark [Finalize Marking, 0.0007422 secs][GC ref-proc, 0.0129203 secs]
[Unloading, 0.0160048 secs], 0.0308670 secs]
```

`-XX:+PrintReferenceGC` reports details for each reference object type at each collection and is very useful for isolating a specific reference object type that the collector is spending the most time processing.

```
[GC remark [Finalize Marking, 0.0003322 secs][GC ref-proc [SoftReference,
2 refs, 0.0052296 secs][WeakReference, 3264308 refs, 2.0524238 secs]
[FinalReference, 215 refs, 0.0028225 secs][PhantomReference, 1787 refs,
0.0050046 secs][JNI Weak Reference, 0.0007776 secs], 2.0932150 secs]
[Unloading, 0.0060031 secs], 2.1201401 secs]
```

Note that G1 is the only HotSpot GC that reports reference processing times with `-XX:+PrintGCDetails`. However, all HotSpot GCs will report per-reference-object-type information using `-XX:+PrintReferenceGC`.

As a general guideline, `Ref Proc` times in `PrintGCDetails` output that are more than 10 percent of the total GC pause time for a G1 young or mixed GC are cause to tune the garbage collector's reference processing. For G1 remark events it is common to see a larger percentage of time spent in reference processing since the remark phase of the concurrent cycle is when the bulk of reference objects discovered during an old generation collection cycle are processed. If the elapsed time for the G1 remark pause exceeds your target pause time and a majority of that time is spent in reference processing, tune as described in the next section.

Reference Processing Tuning

The first thing to do is enable multithreaded reference processing using -XX:+Parallel RefProcEnabled, because HotSpot defaults to single-threaded reference processing. This default exists to minimize memory footprint and to make CPU cycles available to other applications. Enabling this option will burn more CPU during reference processing, but the elapsed, or wall clock, time to complete reference processing will go down.

If reference processing time remains larger than 10 percent of young or mixed GC pause times after adding -XX:+ParallelRefProcEnabled, or G1's remark phase is spending too much time in reference processing, the next step is to determine which reference object type or set of reference object types G1 is spending most of its time processing. -XX:+PrintReferenceGC will report statistics on each reference object type at each GC:

```
[GC pause (young) [SoftReference, 0 refs, 0.0001139 secs][WeakReference,
26845 refs, 0.0050601 secs][FinalReference, 5216 refs, 0.0032409 secs]
[PhantomReference, 336 refs, 0.0000986 secs][JNI Weak Reference, 0.0000836
secs], 0.0726876 secs]
```

A large number of a particular reference object type indicates that the application is heavily using it. Suppose you observe the following:

```
[GC remark [Finalize Marking, 0.0003322 secs][GC ref-proc [SoftReference,
2 refs, 0.0052296 secs][WeakReference, 3264308 refs, 2.0524238 secs]
[FinalReference, 215 refs, 0.0028225 secs][PhantomReference, 1787 refs,
0.0050046 secs][JNI Weak Reference, 0.0007776 secs], 2.0932150 secs]
[Unloading, 0.0060031 secs], 2.1201401 secs]
```

In addition, further suppose you regularly observe a similar pattern of a high number of weak references across other GCs. You can use this information to refactor your application in order to reduce the use of the identified reference object type, or to reduce the reclamation time of that reference object type. In the preceding example, the number of processed weak references is very high relative to the other reference object types, and the amount of time to process them also dominates reference processing time. Corrective actions include the following:

1. Verify that `-XX:+ParallelRefProcEnabled` is enabled. If it is not, enable it and observe whether it reduces pause time enough to reach your pause time goal.

2. If `-XX:+ParallelRefProcEnabled` is enabled, tell the application developers that you are observing a very high weak reference reclamation rate and ask that they consider refactoring the application to reduce the number of weak references being used.

One reference object type to watch for and be careful of using is the soft reference. If `PrintReferenceGC` log output suggests that a large number of soft references are being processed, you may also be observing frequent old generation collection cycles, which consist of concurrent cycles followed by a sequence of mixed GCs. If you see a large number of soft references being processed and GC events are occurring too frequently, or heap occupancy consistently stays near the maximum heap size, tune the aggressiveness with which soft references are reclaimed using `XX:SoftRefLRU PolicyMSPerMB`. It defaults to a value of 1000, and its units are milliseconds.

The default setting of `-XX:SoftRefLRUPolicyMSPerMB=1000` means that a soft reference will be cleared and made eligible for reclamation if the time it was last accessed is greater than 1000ms times the amount of free space in the Java heap, measured in megabytes. To illustrate with an example, suppose `-XX:Soft LRUPolicyMSPerMS=1000`, and the amount of free space is 1GB, that is, 1024MB. Any soft reference that has not been accessed since 1024 × 1000 = 1,024,000ms, or 1024 seconds, or slightly over 17 minutes ago, is eligible to be cleared and reclaimed by the HotSpot garbage collector.

The effect of setting a lower value for `-XX:SoftRefLRUPolicyMSPerMB` is to provoke more aggressive clearing and reclamation of soft references, which leads to lower heap occupancy after GC events, or in other words, less live data. Conversely, setting `-XX:SoftRefLRUPolicyMSPerMB` higher causes less aggressive soft reference clearing and reclamation, which leads to more live data and higher heap occupancy. Tuning `-XX:SoftRefLRUPolicyMSPerMB` may not actually lead to lower reference processing times and in fact may increase them.

The primary reason to tune `-XX:SoftRefLRUPolicyMSPerMB` is to reduce the frequency of old generation collection events by reducing the amount of live data in the heap. We recommend against the use of soft references as a means for implementing memory-sensitive object caches in Java applications because doing so will increase the amount of live data and result in additional GC overheads. See the sidebar "Using Soft References" for more detail.

Using Soft References

It is unfortunate that the soft references JavaDoc (http://docs.oracle.com/javase/8/docs/api/index.html?java/lang/ref/SoftReference.html) recommends their use for implementing memory-sensitive object caches. This often misleads users into thinking that the JVM can manage the size of the object cache and remove entries—that is, free space—as the garbage collector desires or needs. Plus, the existence of -XX:SoftRefLRUPolicyMSPerMB suggests that further control of the object cache is possible. The reality is that the use of soft references for an object cache leads to high heap occupancy, which in turn causes frequent GC events, and in some cases leads to lengthy full GC events or, even worse, out-of-memory errors.

To illustrate why using soft references for object caches tends to result in unexpected or undesirable behavior, let's begin by looking at -XX:SoftLRUPolicyMSPerMB, which tries to control how many recently accessed soft references are kept alive by the garbage collector. For every megabyte of estimated free memory found in the heap before getting rid of the soft references, and after partially figuring out what is no longer reachable (what is dead), the -XX:SoftRefLRUPolicyMSPerMB value in milliseconds is added to a time window of how long it has been since the application accessed a given reference's soft reference yes/no test for keeping it strongly alive in a currently executing garbage collection.

If you step back and think about what this means, the faster an application runs, the more frequently you can expect soft references to be accessed. For example, say an application is executing 10,000 transactions per second. That application is accessing 100 times more soft references per second than if it were executing 100 transactions per second. The object allocation and promotion rates are also roughly 100 times greater. The faster the application executes, the harder it makes the garbage collector work.

Keep in mind that the amount of free megabytes used to estimate the "which soft references to keep" time window is computed based on how much space will be free if all soft references were to be cleared and reclaimed. However, the garbage collector has no way of knowing how much additional memory will be kept alive by a soft reference. It can only speculate or make an estimate of how many soft references to keep alive without knowing how much memory they will actually retain.

Also, the larger the number of soft references that are kept alive, say in an object cache, the less actual free memory will remain at the end of a garbage collection. The less the amount of space available after a GC, the more frequently the garbage collector will run for a given allocation or promotion rate. For example, at ten times less free memory, the garbage collector will run ten times more frequently and will do approximately ten times more work per some unit of application work.

What this means is that soft references are useful when an application is doing little or no work, because the overhead of soft reference use grows at the square of the rate of application work. You can control the constant multiplier ahead of that square, but that is the only control you have. This is why many GC tuning guides suggest setting this constant multiplier to zero using -XX:SoftLRUPolicyMSPerMB=0.

Keep in mind there is no Java or JVM specification that specifies a default value for the constant multiplier just described. A garbage collector implementation can clear and reclaim a differing number of soft references for the same Java application executing with the same size Java heap with the same load. This means that if you are using soft references for a memory-sensitive object cache, the size of that object cache may vary between garbage collectors, not only between different JVM vendors, but also from one garbage collector to another within the same JVM. You may observe completely different GC behavior such as a difference in live data or heap occupancy, number of GCs, the frequency at which they occur, and/or their duration by moving between HotSpot's CMS, Parallel, and G1 GCs. JVMs such as IBM's J9 or Azul's Zing may also behave differently with respect to soft reference reclamation. This puts limitations on the portability of a Java application using soft references since it will behave differently moving from one garbage collector to another, or at least require JVM tuning of the constant multiplier, which may be nontrivial, in order to achieve acceptable application behavior.

References

[1] Charlie Hunt and Binu John. *Java™ Performance*. Addison-Wesley, Upper Saddle River, NJ, 2012. ISBN 978-0-13-714252-1.

[2] Nirmar S. Arora, Robert D. Blumofe, and C. Greg Plaxton. "Thread Scheduling for Multiprogrammed Multiprocessors." *Proceedings of the Tenth Annual ACM Symposium on Parallel Algorithms and Architectures*. ACM, New York, 1998, pp. 119–29. ISBN 0-89791-989-0.

4

The Serviceability Agent

Debugging and troubleshooting tools play an important role in the development of well-performing Java applications. There are many tools available to debug applications at the Java level, but very few are available for troubleshooting problems in Java applications at the JVM level. This chapter talks in detail about a powerful set of debugging tools called the Serviceability Agent (SA) that can help in debugging Java applications at the Java as well as the JVM level. The SA has the ability to debug live Java processes as well as core files, also called crash dump files.

In this chapter, we will take a look at what the Serviceability Agent is, where we can get it, and what we can do with its set of tools.

For building high-performance Java applications, it is a must that those applications be free from various problems that an application can encounter. Those problems could be application hangs, memory leaks, unexpected application behavior, and crashes. The Serviceability Agent's set of tools can greatly help in troubleshooting and nailing down those problems, resulting in stable, reliable, scalable, and efficient Java applications.

The Serviceability Agent is very useful in debugging core files or crash dump files. As we all know, core or crash dump files contain the complete state of a program at a specific time such as the state of memory, processor registers, stack information, and other processor and operating system flag information. The Serviceability Agent has the capability to read the core files of the Java HotSpot Virtual Machine (HotSpot VM) and present the details from it in a human-readable format.

What Is the Serviceability Agent?

The HotSpot Serviceability Agent is a hidden treasure present in the JDK that very few people know about. It is a set of Java APIs and tools that can be used to debug live Java processes and core files (aka crash dumps on Windows). The SA can examine Java processes or core files, which makes it suitable for debugging Java programs as well as the HotSpot VM. It is a snapshot debugger that lets us look at the state of a frozen Java process or a core file. When the SA is attached to a Java process, it stops the process at that point so that we can explore the Java heap, look at the threads that were running in the process at that point, examine internal data structures of the HotSpot VM, and look at the loaded classes, compiled code of methods, and so on. The process resumes after the SA is detached from it.

As mentioned before, the SA is a snapshot debugger, which means that it works with the snapshot of a process, unlike the usual debuggers that provide the facility to step through a running program.

Note that the SA runs in a separate process from the target process and executes no code in the target process. However, the target process is halted while the SA observes it.

Why Do We Need the SA?

Why use the SA when we have native debugging tools like dbx, gdb, WinDbg, and many others available on all the platforms?

First, the SA is a Java-based platform-independent tool, so it can be used to debug Java processes/cores on all the platforms where Java is supported. Additionally, debugging a Java process or the Java HotSpot Virtual Machine with native debuggers is very limiting as they can help us examine the native OS process state but not the Java or the JVM state of the process. For example, if we need to view the objects in the Java heap, native debuggers would show us the raw hex numbers, whereas the SA has the ability to interpret those hex numbers and present the object view instead. The SA has the knowledge about the Java heap, its boundaries, objects in the Java heap, loaded classes, thread objects, and internal data structures of the Java HotSpot Virtual Machine. Empowered with this knowledge, the SA makes it very easy for us to examine the Java/JVM-level details of the Java process or core.

SA Components

The SA consists mostly of Java classes, but it also contains a small amount of native code to read raw bits from the processes and the core files:

- On Solaris, SA uses `libproc` to read bits from a process or a core file.
- On Linux, SA uses a mix of `/proc` and `ptrace` (mostly the latter) to read bits from a process. For core files, SA parses Executable and Linkable Format (ELF) files directly.
- On Windows, SA uses the Windows Debugger Engine interface (dbgeng.dll library) to read the raw bits from the processes and core files.

SA Binaries in the JDK

There are two binaries present in the JDK that make up the SA. These binaries are shipped with the JDK:

- sa-jdi.jar
- sawindbg.dll on Windows, libsaproc.so on Solaris/Linux

SA components are built as part of the standard build of the HotSpot repository. The native code component of SA is placed in libsaproc.so or sawindbg.dll, and the Java classes are placed in sa-jdi.jar.

The binary sa-jdi.jar provides the SA Java APIs and also includes useful debugging tools implemented using these APIs. It also includes an implementation of the Java Debug Interface (JDI), which allows JDI clients to do read-only debugging on core files and hung processes.

JDK Versions with Complete SA Binaries

SA binaries are shipped with the following JDK releases:

- JDK 7, and later releases on all platforms
- JDK 6u17+ on Solaris and Linux
- JDK 6u31+ on Windows

Prior to these versions, the SA was not shipped with the JDK on Windows, and only a subset of SA classes was shipped with JDKs on Solaris and Linux. The JDK versions listed make the complete set of SA classes available on all of these platforms.

How the SA Understands HotSpot VM Data Structures

There is a file src/share/vm/runtime/vmStructs.cpp in the HotSpot source base that defines a VMStructs class that contains declarations of each HotSpot class and its fields, as well as the declarations of the processor-dependent items such as registers, sizeof types, and so on. The SA understands the Java objects and HotSpot data structures with the help of the declarations in this file.

As an example, in the file src/share/vm/oops/cpCacheOop.hpp we have the following:

```
:
class constantPoolCacheOopDesc: public arrayOopDesc {
  friend class VMStructs;
  private:
    // the corresponding constant pool
    constantPoolOop _constant_pool;
:
```

In vmStructs.cpp, the _constant_pool field is declared as

```
nonstatic_field(constantPoolCacheOopDesc, _constant_pool,
constantPoolOop)
```

From the _constant_pool field in the file vmStructs.cpp, the SA knows there is a class named constantPoolCacheOopDesc that has a field with the name _constant_pool of type constantPoolOop in the Java HotSpot VM.

HotSpot Data Structure Definitions

There are a couple of additional noteworthy definitions to explain here. A constant pool is a table of structures representing various numeric and string constants, class and interface names, field names, and other constants that are referred to within the class and its subclasses, and an oop (ordinary object pointer) is a memory address pointing to an instance of an internal HotSpot data structure that represents a Java object.

Note that VMStructs is declared as a friend class. Most of the classes in HotSpot declare VMStructs to be a friend so that the private fields of that class can be accessed in VMStructs.

During the HotSpot build, vmStructs.cpp is compiled into vmStructs.o, which is included in the shared library libjvm.so or jvm.dll. vmStructs.o contains all the data that the SA needs to read the HotSpot data internal representations. And at runtime, the SA can read this data from the target VM.

The structure and field names declared in vmStructs.cpp are used by the corresponding Java code in the SA. Thus, if a field named in vmStructs.cpp is deleted or renamed, the corresponding Java code that accesses that field also needs to be modified. If declarations in VMStructs and the Java code in SA are not in sync, SA will fail when it tries to examine a process/core file.

SA Version Matching

As we saw in the previous section, the Java code in SA is a mirror of the C++ code in HotSpot. If some data structures or algorithms are changed, added, or removed in HotSpot, the same changes have to be made in the SA Java code. Due to this tight coupling between the SA Java code and the HotSpot implementation, an SA instance can reliably debug only the HotSpot VM that was built from the same repository as that of the SA instance. In order to detect the version mismatch between the SA and the target HotSpot, we place a file named sa.properties into sa-jdi.jar during the HotSpot build process. This file contains an SA version property, for example,

```
sun.jvm.hotspot.runtime.VM.saBuildVersion=24.0-b56
```

At runtime, SA reads this property, compares it with the version of the target HotSpot VM being analyzed, and throws a VMVersionMismatchException if the versions do not match. This check can be disabled by running the SA tools with the following system property:

```
-Dsun.jvm.hotspot.runtime.VM.disableVersionCheck
```

With this option, SA does not complain if its version does not match the version of the target VM and attempts to attach to it. This option is useful if you want to attach the SA to a non-matching version of the target HotSpot VM.

The Serviceability Agent Debugging Tools

There are two main SA debugging tools that are implemented using the Serviceability Agent APIs: HotSpot Debugger (HSDB) and Command-Line HotSpot Debugger (CLHSDB). HSDB is the top-level GUI program offering many visual utilities that help in debugging the HotSpot VM. CLHSDB is the command-line variant of HSDB. When debugging remote core dumps, it is much easier to work with the command-line HSDB than with the GUI HSDB tool.

HSDB

HotSpot Debugger is the main GUI tool. It facilitates examining a Java process, core file, and also a remote Java process. Let's see how we can launch and use it on a Windows machine.

First, let's set the JAVA_HOME environment variable to the folder where the JDK that we want to use is installed so that we can use this variable wherever we need to access files/folders in that JDK:

```
set JAVA_HOME=d:\Java\7u40
```

On Windows, the PATH environment variable should contain the location of the JVM binary used by the target process/core and also the folder where Microsoft Debugging Tools for Windows is installed on the machine, for example:

```
set PATH=%JAVA_HOME%\bin\server;d:\windbg;%PATH%
```

Now we can launch HSDB using the following command:

```
%JAVA_HOME%\bin\java -classpath%JAVA_HOME%\lib\sa-jdi.jar
sun.jvm.hotspot.HSDB
```

On Solaris and Linux, we just need to set JAVA_HOME to point to the installed JDK and then launch the tool as in the following:

```
$JAVA_HOME/bin/java -classpath $JAVA_HOME/lib/sa-jdi.jar sun.jvm.hotspot.
HSDB
```

These launch commands bring up the HSDB GUI tool as shown in Figure 4.1.

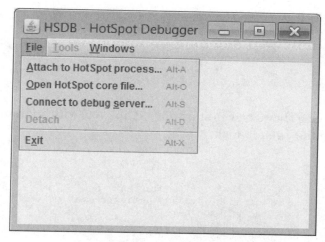

Figure 4.1 HSDB GUI

Beginning with JDK 9, there are two different ways to launch HSDB. For instance, here is an example of how to launch the SA with JDK 9:

```
set PATH=d:\Java\jdk9-b102\bin;%PATH%
java sun.jvm.hotspot.HSDB
```

This brings up HSDB.

JDK 9 also contains a jhsdb executable in JDK 9's bin directory that can be used to launch various SA tools. For example:

```
set PATH=d:\Java\jdk9-b102\bin;%PATH%
jhsdb.exe
    clhsdb              command line debugger
    hsdb               ui debugger
    jstack --help      to get more information
    jmap   --help      to get more information
    jinfo  --help      to get more information
```

jhsdb.exe with no arguments offers help by showing additional arguments that can be passed to jhsdb to launch various SA tools. For example:

```
jhsdb.exe hsdb
```

This brings up the HSDB GUI debugger.

The following will start the command-line debugger:

```
jhsdb.exe clhsdb
hsdb>
```

And the following shows how to start the jstack tool with additional options that can be passed to the jstack tool:

```
jhsdb.exe jstack
    --locks     to print java.util.concurrent locks
    --mixed     to print both java and native frames (mixed mode)
    --exe       executable image name
    --core      path to coredump
    --pid       pid of process to attach
```

Serviceability Agent Debugging Modes

There are three ways in which the HSDB can attach to the target HotSpot VM:

- Attach to a local HotSpot process
- Attach to a core file
- Attach to a remote debug server

Attach to a HotSpot Process

HSDB provides a facility to attach to a running Java process. Click File >Attach to HotSpot process and it brings up a dialog box that asks for the ID of the process to which we want to attach the SA, as shown in Figure 4.2.

After typing the process ID, click OK and SA gets attached to the process. The process is paused at this point and remains paused as long as SA is attached to it. Recall that SA is a snapshot debugger and provides a snapshot view of the process at the point in time when it is attached to the process. Figure 4.3 shows the HSDB main window after the SA gets attached to the process.

After analyzing the process, when we detach SA from the process, the process resumes its execution normally. The action of detaching the SA from the process is shown in Figure 4.4.

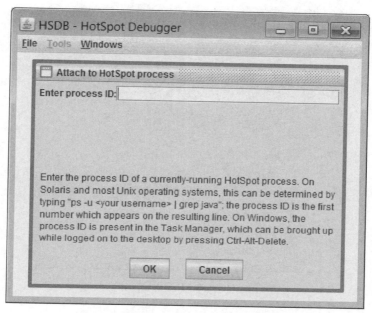

Figure 4.2 Attach to HotSpot process

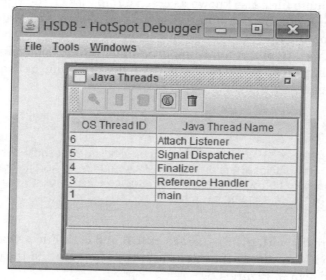

Figure 4.3 HSDB main window

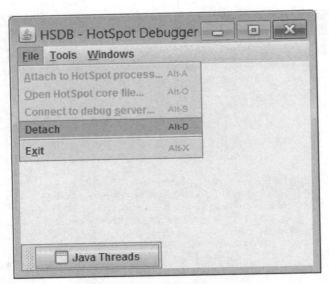

Figure 4.4 HSDB Detach

Attach to HotSpot Core Files

SA is a very useful tool for postmortem analysis. With SA, it is possible to attach to HotSpot "core" dump files, also known as crash dump files on the Windows platform. A core or crash dump file is a binary file that consists of the state of a running program at a specific time. Core files may be generated due to process crashes, or they can be dumped from a running application for offline debugging. More details on core/crash dump files are covered in the section "Core Dump or Crash Dump Files" later in the chapter.

> **Tip**
>
> Note that the HotSpot core/crash dump file can be very large depending on the amount of state information it contains at the time of core/crash dump file generation. You may have to configure the operating system to generate large core files and also ensure that the file system where the file is generated has sufficient space.

To open a core file with the SA, launch HSDB and click File > Open HotSpot core file as shown in Figure 4.5. Then, enter the path to the core and the path to the Java executable as shown in Figure 4.6.

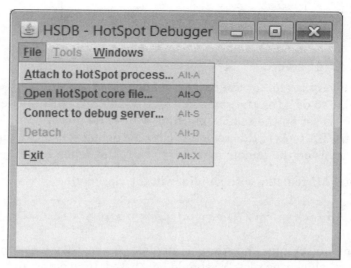

Figure 4.5 HSDB File options

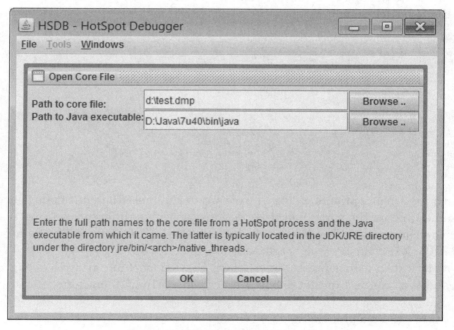

Figure 4.6 HSDB Open Core File

After attaching to the core file, HSDB provides the same set of tools to explore the core as it does with the live process.

Connect to Debug Server

This feature is very useful for the remote debugging of processes or core files when it is not possible to do so on the same machine as the SA. With this feature, we can run the debug server on the remote machine where the process/core is present and then connect the SA tools to this remotely running debug server. We need to perform the following steps on the remote machine to start the debug server:

1. Start the RMI registry with sa-jdi.jar in the classpath:

```
$JAVA_HOME/bin/rmiregistry -J-Xbootclasspath/p:${JAVA_HOME}/lib/sa-jdi.jar
```

This command creates and starts a remote object registry. One can specify a port number at which this registry should be started. If no port number is specified, the registry is started on port 1099.

2. Start the debug server on the remote machine, specifying the process or core file to be debugged:

```
${JAVA_HOME}/bin/java -classpath $JAVA_HOME/lib/sa-jdi.jar
  sun.jvm.hotspot.DebugServer <pid> [uniqueID]
```

or

```
${JAVA_HOME}/bin/java -classpath ${JAVA_HOME}/lib/sa-jdi.jar
sun.jvm.hotspot.DebugServer
<pathname to the java executable that produced the core file>
<pathname of the corefile to debug> [uniqueID]
```

uniqueID is an optional string. If we want to run more than one debug server at the same time on the same machine, we must specify a different uniqueID string for each debug server. The debug server starts the RMI registry at the default port 1099 if the RMI registry was not already started.

Now, let's start a Java process on a Solaris SPARC machine, attach a debug server to it, and then connect to that debug server from a Windows machine.

1. Start the Java process:

```
myserver% java TestClass &
27813
```

2. Start rmiregistry and the debug server:

```
myserver% rmiregistry -J-Xbootclasspath/p:$JAVA_HOME/lib/sa-jdi.jar
```

3. Start the debug server, passing it the HotSpot process ID and the unique name we want to assign to this debuggee:

```
myserver% $JAVA_HOME/bin/java -cp $JAVA_HOME/lib/sa-jdi.jar
-Djava.rmi.server.codebase=file:/$JAVA_HOME/lib/sa-jdi.jar
 sun.jvm.hotspot.DebugServer 27813 1234
Attaching to process ID 27813 and starting RMI services, please
wait...
Debugger attached and RMI services started.
```

From the Windows machine, we can now connect to this specific debug server using the unique identifier and the hostname in *[uniqueID@]hostname* format as shown in Figure 4.7. Once the unique ID and hostname have been entered and the OK button has been pressed, the SA will display a status window saying it is trying to connect to the debug server, as shown in Figure 4.8.

After connecting the HSDB to the debug server, we can use all the utilities available under the Tools menu and debug the process as if it were running on our local machine.

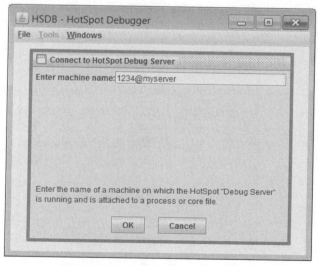

Figure 4.7 Connect to HotSpot Debug Server

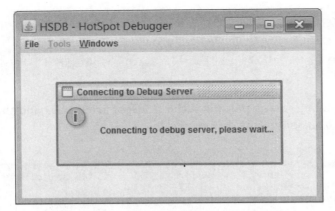

Figure 4.8 Connecting to Debug Server

HSDB Tools

HSDB offers many utilities that help us explore and debug Java processes or core files.

Java Threads

The first window that appears in HSDB when it is connected to a Java process or core file is the panel that displays all the Java threads in the target JVM. Figure 4.9 shows all the Java threads in the attached Java process.

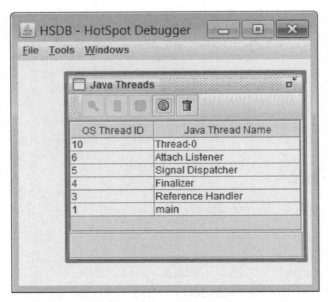

Figure 4.9 Java Threads

This panel has some interesting icons at the top left to show information on the selected Java thread:

- Inspect Thread: This icon brings up the Object Inspector window showing the VM representation of the thread object. See Figure 4.10.
- Show Stack Memory: This shows the stack data with symbol information at the stack memory of the selected thread as in Figure 4.11.

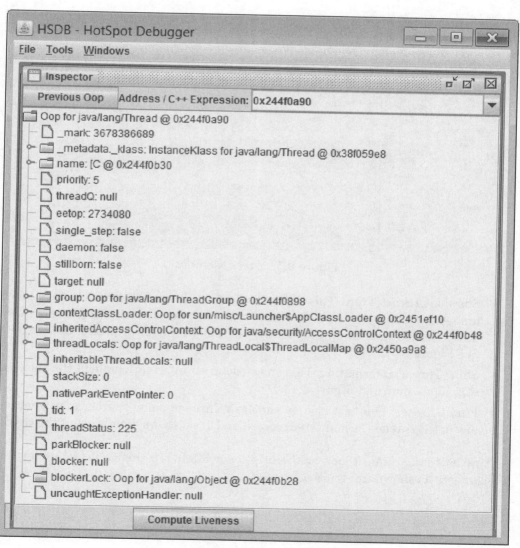

Figure 4.10 Inspector

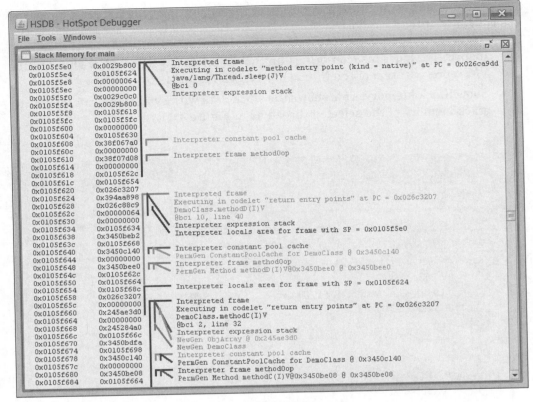

Figure 4.11 Stack Memory

- Show Java Stack Trace: This shows the Java stack trace of a thread. The method names and addresses are hyperlinks in the displayed stack trace, and clicking these method links shows the method details in the lower part of the window. See Figure 4.12.
- Show Thread Information: This shows detailed information about the selected thread, as shown in Figure 4.13.
- Find Crashes: This last icon on the Java Threads panel searches for whether any of the threads encountered a crash and, if so, shows details about the crash.

Now let's take a quick look at the utilities available in this GUI tool under the Tools menu, as shown in Figure 4.14.

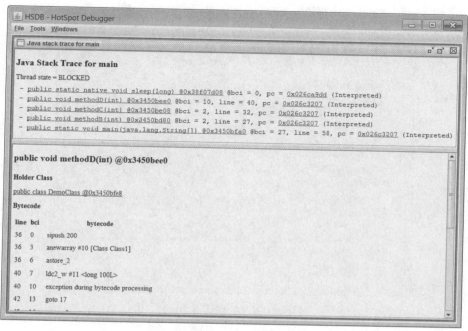

Figure 4.12 Java Stack Trace

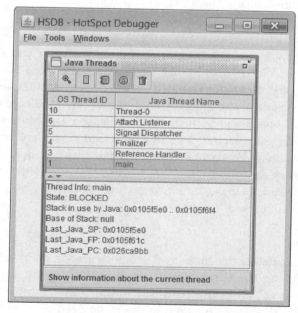

Figure 4.13 Thread information

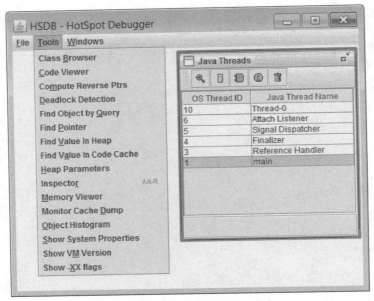

Figure 4.14 HSDB Tools

Some of these tools are helpful in debugging the Java-level issues, and some are very useful in troubleshooting the JVM-level problems.

Class Browser

With the Class Browser (see the example in Figure 4.15), we can see all the classes loaded by the target VM. It also allows us to dump the class files for all or some selective classes loaded in the target VM. This tool is very useful when we do not have access to the source code of the application and just have the core dump file and we need to investigate some issue with the loaded classes. For example, if some loaded class is not behaving as expected, we can dump that class, look at its code, and try to figure out the problem. Or perhaps there are too many loaded classes and we are getting out-of-memory errors; with the Class Browser we can look through the classes and see if some unneeded classes are also getting loaded or whether the classes are getting unloaded as expected.

Deadlock Detection

This feature helps us detect the Java-level deadlock among the threads. If a Java-level deadlock exists among the threads in the target VM, this tool prints information about the threads involved in the deadlock and also the monitors they are waiting to acquire. Figure 4.16 shows an example where no deadlocks were found.

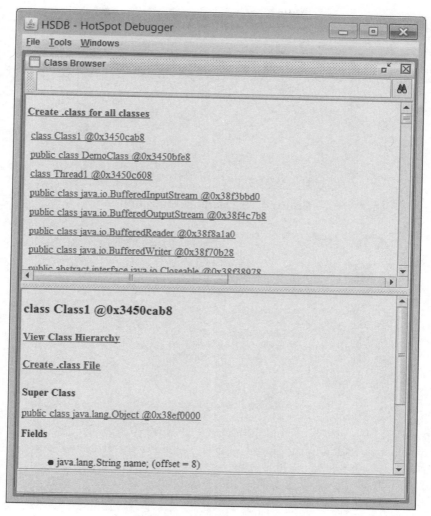

Figure 4.15 Class Browser

Object Inspector

We can inspect the Java objects as well as the VM internal C++ structures using the Object Inspector tool.

To inspect a Java object, we need to provide the object's address in the Java heap; this tool shows the internal fields of the object as in Figure 4.17.

Object Inspector can also show the VM internal C++ structures that are described by the VMStructs database in the target VM. See Figure 4.18.

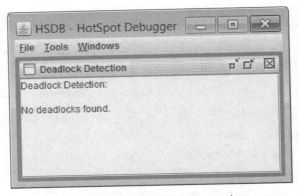

Figure 4.16 Deadlock Detection

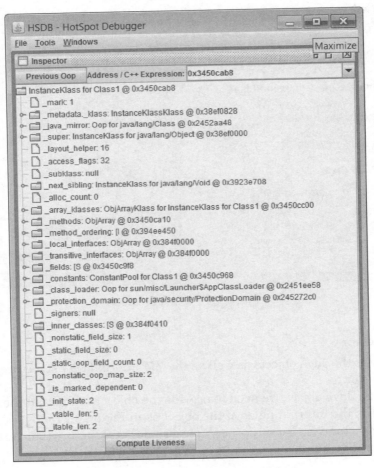

Figure 4.17 Inspector—Java object

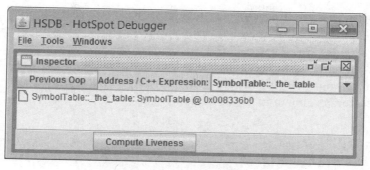

Figure 4.18 Inspector—VM structures

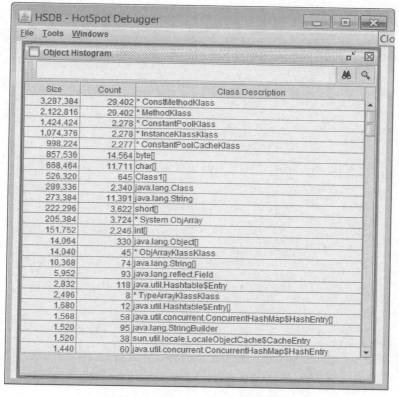

Figure 4.19 Object Histogram

Object Histogram

With the Object Histogram tool, an example of which is shown in Figure 4.19, we can get a histogram of the objects present in the Java heap. This tool helps in diagnosing memory leaks or out-of-memory-related problems in Java programs.

This tool also has a feature to show the instances of a particular class. Clicking on the search icon in the top right corner brings up the window showing all the instances of the selected class. See Figure 4.20.

We can select any instance from the list of instances and get the liveness path of the object through which that object is reachable and is considered alive by the garbage collector, as shown in Figure 4.21.

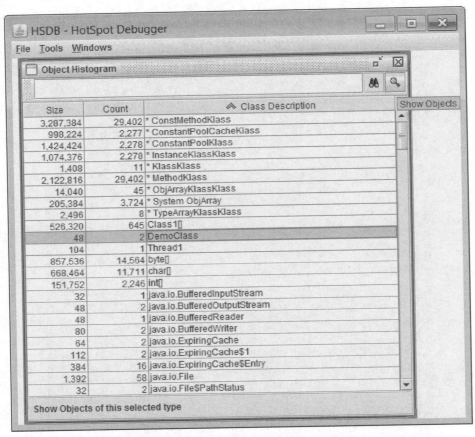

Figure 4.20 Histogram—Show Objects

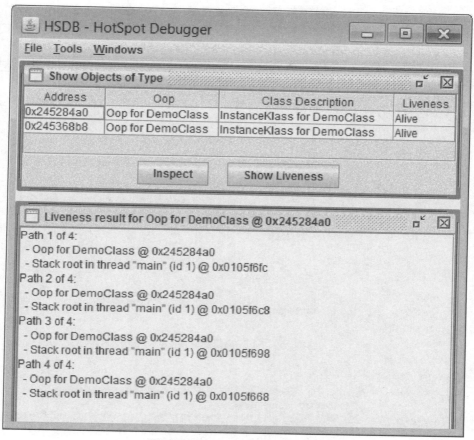

Figure 4.21 Show Liveness

Compute Reverse Pointers

This utility computes the reference paths through which an object is reachable from the GC roots—the reference paths that are responsible for keeping that object alive in the Java heap. Once we have computed the reverse pointers, the `<<Reverse pointers>>` field in the Object Inspector window for an object shows the reverse pointers through which that object is reachable, as shown in Figure 4.22.

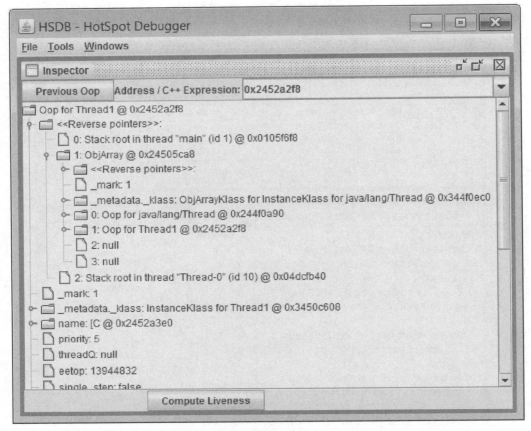

Figure 4.22 Reverse pointers

We can also see the liveness path of the object in another window by using the Compute Liveness and Show Liveness buttons available in the Inspector window. See Figure 4.23.

Find Object by Query

This tool provides an SQL-based query language to query Java objects from the Java heap; for example, to find all the thread objects in the Java heap, we can execute a query like this:

```
select t from java.lang.Thread t
```

Figure 4.24 shows the result of executing this query.

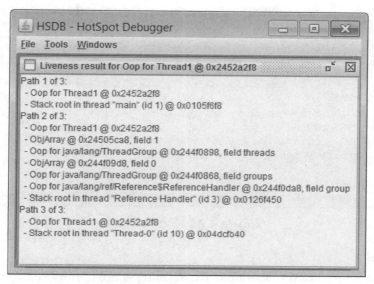

Figure 4.23 Liveness result

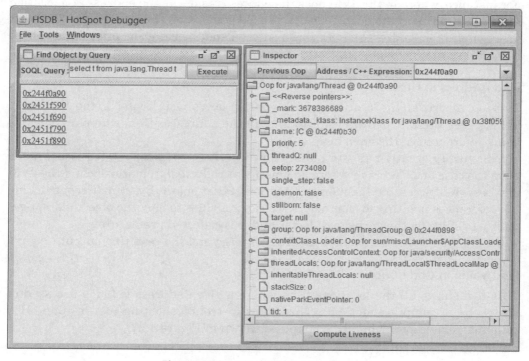

Figure 4.24 Find Object by Query

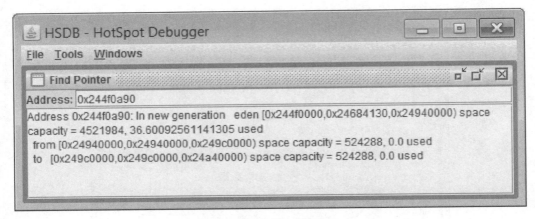

Figure 4.25 Find Pointer

Find Pointer

This tool can help us find where a particular address lies in the Java process address space. This is particularly useful when we are dealing with JVM crashes and want to know the details of the memory address being accessed when the JVM crashed. For instance, where in the JVM does the address reside? Is the address at a location in the Java heap, in the eden space, in the old generation space? Figure 4.25 shows an example of an address that has been entered and the resulting information about the address that is displayed.

Find Address in Heap

This tool reports all the locations where a particular value is located in the Java heap. This is very useful when we want to find all the addresses from where an object is being referenced in the Java heap.

This utility greatly helps in nailing down garbage-collector-related issues, such as in the case of a GC crash where an object was collected prematurely and the JVM crashes while accessing the memory location of that object. By transitively tracking the references pointing to that object, we can get clues to why the object did not get marked as live by the garbage collector and was collected prematurely.

Figure 4.26 shows an example address entered and the resulting output.

Find Value in Code Cache

This tool shows all the locations from where a given address is being accessed in the cache of compiled methods. This helps in troubleshooting just-in-time (JIT) compiler-related problems. An example is shown in Figure 4.27.

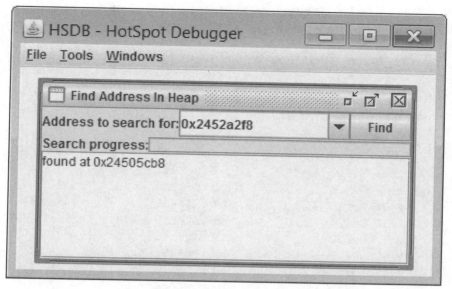

Figure 4.26 Find Address in Heap

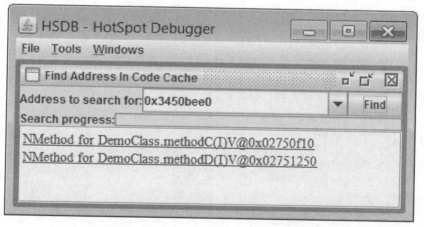

Figure 4.27 Find Value in Code Cache

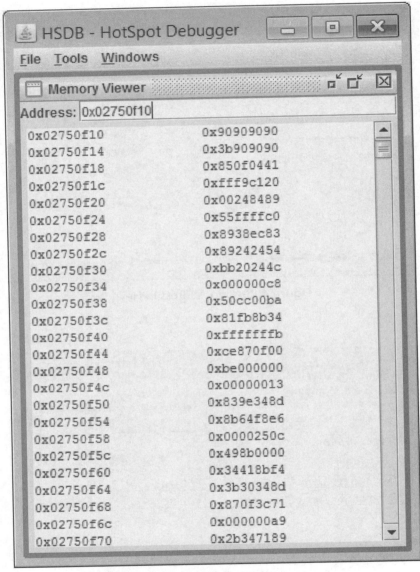

Figure 4.28 Memory Viewer

Memory Viewer

Memory Viewer shows the raw memory contents in hexadecimal format at any given heap address. See Figure 4.28.

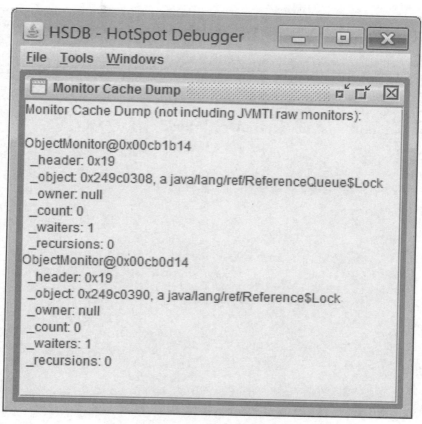

Figure 4.29 Monitor Cache Dump

Monitor Cache Dump

This utility dumps the cache of object monitors as shown in Figure 4.29. This is useful in troubleshooting synchronization-related issues.

Code Viewer

Code Viewer (see the example in Figure 4.30) can show us the bytecodes of a method and the JIT compiler-generated machine code of the method if the method has been compiled. This tool is very useful in troubleshooting JIT compiler issues. Many times we encounter problems where a certain method compiled by the server/client compiler is either producing unexpected results or is causing a JVM crash. By looking at the disassembled generated compiled code (see Figure 4.31), we can get to the root of such issues.

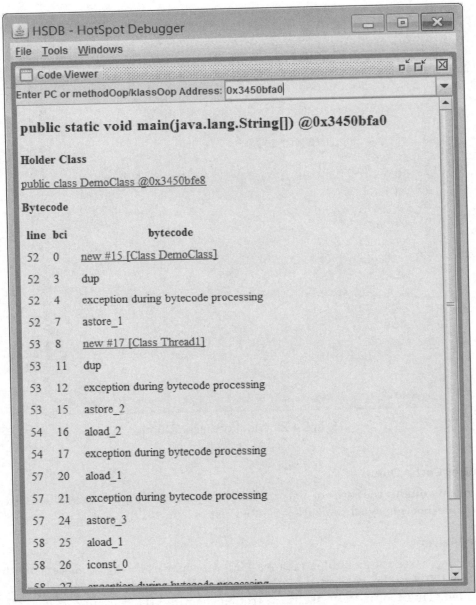

Figure 4.30 Bytecodes of the interpreted method

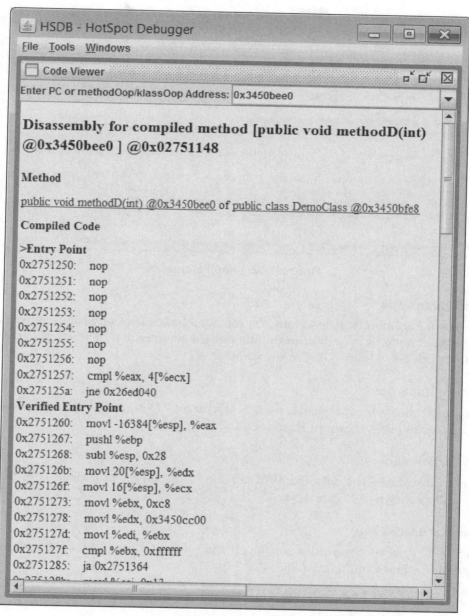

Figure 4.31 Generated code of the compiled code

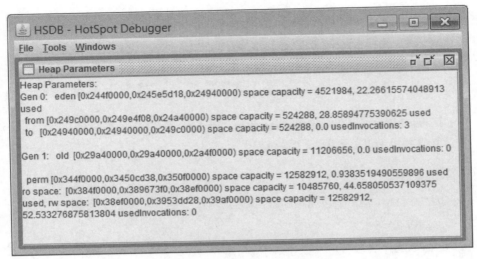

Figure 4.32 Heap Parameters

Heap Parameters

The Heap Parameters utility shows us the heap boundaries of various generations of the Java heap. It is helpful in finding out the heap region in which a particular address lies. See Figure 4.32 for an example.

System Properties

We can get the system properties used by the target VM using the System Properties tool. An example is shown in Figure 4.33.

VM Version Info

This utility shows the detailed JVM version of the target process or core file. An example is shown in Figure 4.34.

Command Line Flags

This utility shows the values set for all the command-line -XX JVM options. An example is shown in Figure 4.35.

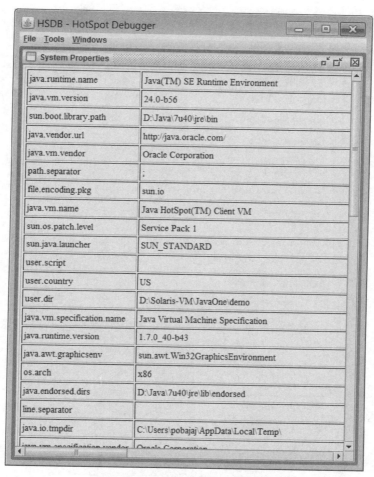

Figure 4.33 System Properties

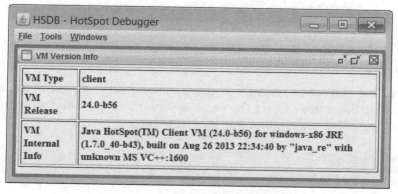

Figure 4.34 VM Version Info

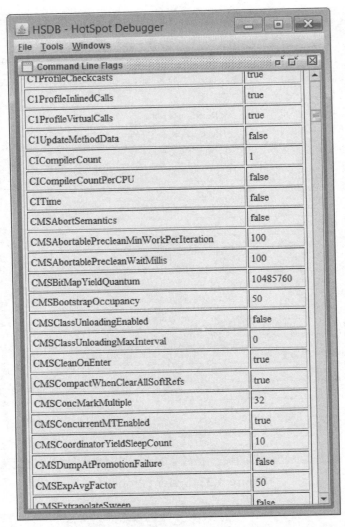

Figure 4.35 Command Line Flags

CLHSDB

Command-Line HotSpot Debugger is the command-line variant of the HSDB. To launch CLHSDB, we need to set the same environment variables as we did for the HSDB. Use the following command to launch this tool:

```
$JAVA_HOME/bin/java -classpath $JAVA_HOME/lib/sa-jdi.jar
sun.jvm.hotspot.CLHSDB
```

It offers almost all the features that the UI version of the tool does; for example, to examine any Java object or VM data structure there is a command called `inspect`:

```
hsdb> inspect 0x23f50a20
instance of Oop for java/lang/Thread @ 0x23f50a20 @ 0x23f50a20 (size = 104)
_mark: 1
_metadata._klass: InstanceKlass for java/lang/Thread @ 0x38966700 Oop @
0x38966700
name: [C @ 0x23f50ac0 Oop for [C @ 0x23f50ac0
priority: 5
threadQ: null null
eetop: 4758528
single_step: false
daemon: false
stillborn: false
target: null null
group: Oop for java/lang/ThreadGroup @ 0x23f50840 Oop for java/lang/
ThreadGroup @ 0x23f50840
contextClassLoader: Oop for sun/misc/Launcher$AppClassLoader @ 0x23f7b398
Oop for sun/misc/Launcher$AppClassLoader @ 0x23f7b398
inheritedAccessControlContext: Oop for java/security/AccessControlContext
@ 0x23f50ad8 Oop for java/security/AccessControlContext @ 0x23f50ad8
threadLocals: Oop for java/lang/ThreadLocal$ThreadLocalMap @ 0x23f7c960
Oop for java/lang/ThreadLocal$ThreadLocalMap @ 0x23f7c960
inheritableThreadLocals: null null
stackSize: 0
nativeParkEventPointer: 0
tid: 1
threadStatus: 5
parkBlocker: null null
blocker: null null
blockerLock: Oop for java/lang/Object @ 0x23f50ab8 Oop for java/lang/
Object @ 0x23f50ab8
uncaughtExceptionHandler: null nullCheck heap boundaries
```

To get the heap boundaries, we can use the command `universe`:

```
hsdb> universe
Heap Parameters:
Gen 0:    eden [0x23f50000,0x23fae5a0,0x243a0000) space capacity = 4521984,
8.546337182971014 used
   from [0x243a0000,0x243a0000,0x24420000) space capacity = 524288, 0.0
used
   to   [0x24420000,0x24420000,0x244a0000) space capacity = 524288, 0.0
usedInvocations: 0
Gen 1:    old [0x294a0000,0x294a0000,0x29f50000) space capacity =
11206656, 0.0 usedInvocations: 0
   perm [0x33f50000,0x33f68700,0x34b50000) space capacity = 12582912,
0.7954915364583334 used   ro space:   [0x37f50000,0x383d2e40,0x38950000)
space capacity = 10485760, 45.1129150390625 used, rw space:
[0x38950000,0x38fd67b8,0x39550000) space capacity = 12582912,
54.37768300374349 usedInvocations: 0
```

List of Commands

Here is the complete list of commands available with the CLHSDB tool:

```
hsdb> help
Available commands:
  assert true | false
  attach pid | exec core
  detach
  dumpcfg { -a | id }
  dumpcodecache
  dumpideal { -a | id }
  dumpilt { -a | id }
  echo [ true | false ]
  examine [ address/count ] | [ address,address]
  field [ type [ name fieldtype isStatic offset address ] ]
  findpc address
  flags [ flag | -nd ]
  help [ command ]
  history
  inspect expression
  intConstant [ name [ value ] ]
  jhisto
  jstack [-v]
  livenmethods
  longConstant [ name [ value ] ]
  pmap
  print expression
  printas type expression
  printmdo [ -a | expression ]
  printstatics [ type ]
  pstack [-v]
  quit
  reattach
  revptrs address
  scanoops start end [ type ]
  search [ heap | perm | rawheap | codecache | threads ] value
  source filename
  symbol address
  symboldump
  symboltable name
  thread { -a | id }
  threads
  tokenize ...
  type [ type [ name super isOop isInteger isUnsigned size ] ]
  universe
  verbose true | false
  versioncheck [ true | false ]
  vmstructsdump
  where { -a | id }
```

Some Other Tools

Some more very handy, small utilities are bundled with the SA. These tools can be attached to a process, to a core file, or to a remote debug server. Let's take a look at how we can use them and what useful information they provide.

FinalizerInfo

This tool prints details on the finalizable objects in the target VM:

```
java -classpath %JAVA_HOME%\lib\sa-jdi.jar
sun.jvm.hotspot.tools.FinalizerInfo 5684
Attaching to process ID 5684, please wait...
Debugger attached successfully.
Client compiler detected.
JVM version is 24.0-b56
Number of objects pending for finalization: 0
```

HeapDumper

This tool can dump the Java heap to a file in the hprof format:

```
java -classpath %JAVA_HOME%\lib\sa-jdi.jar
sun.jvm.hotspot.tools.HeapDumper 5684
Attaching to process ID 5684, please wait...
Debugger attached successfully.
Client compiler detected.
JVM version is 24.0-b56
Dumping heap to heap.bin ...
Heap dump file created
```

PermStat

This tool prints the statistics of the permanent generation of the attached process or the core file:

```
java -classpath %JAVA_HOME%\lib\sa-jdi.jar
sun.jvm.hotspot.tools.PermStat 5684
Attaching to process ID 5684, please wait...
Debugger attached successfully.
Client compiler detected.
JVM version is 24.0-b56
10713 intern Strings occupying 802608 bytes.
finding class loader instances ..
done.
computing per loader stat ..done.
please wait.. computing
liveness..............................................done.
```

Continued

```
class_loader          classes  bytes    parent_loader   alive?  type
<bootstrap>           342      1539808  null            live    <internal>
0x23f7b398            3        28016    0x23f762e0      live
sun/misc/Launcher$AppClassLoader@0x38a0e9c0
0x23f762e0            0        0        null            live
sun/misc/Launcher$ExtClassLoader@0x389eb420

total = 3             345      1567824  N/A             alive=3, dead=0   N/A
```

PMap

This tool prints the process map of the target process/core much like the Solaris
pmap tool:

```
java -classpath %JAVA_HOME%\lib\sa-jdi.jar sun.jvm.hotspot.tools.PMap 5684
Attaching to process ID 5684, please wait...
Debugger attached successfully.
Client compiler detected.
JVM version is 24.0-b56
0x011c0000      184K     d:\java\7u40\bin\java.exe
0x6c0f0000      3232K    d:\java\7u40\jre\bin\client\jvm.dll
0x6f5c0000      200K     C:\windows\system32\WINMM.dll
0x70900000      760K     d:\java\7u40\jre\bin\msvcr100.dll
0x74220000      1656K    C:\windows\WinSxS\x86_microsoft.windows.common-
controls_6595b64144ccf1df_6.0.7601.17514_none_41e6975e2bd6f2b2\COMCTL32.dll
0x74990000      28K      C:\windows\system32\WSOCK32.dll
0x74b20000      76K      d:\java\7u40\jre\bin\zip.dll
0x74b40000      128K     d:\java\7u40\jre\bin\java.dll
0x74b60000      48K      d:\java\7u40\jre\bin\verify.dll
0x74cc0000      48K      C:\windows\syswow64\CRYPTBASE.dll
0x74cd0000      384K     C:\windows\syswow64\SspiCli.dll
0x74d30000      212K     C:\windows\syswow64\WS2_32.dll
0x74d70000      1088K    C:\windows\syswow64\kernel32.dll
0x74fa0000      628K     C:\windows\syswow64\USP10.dll
0x75cc0000      640K     C:\windows\syswow64\ADVAPI32.dll
0x75ff0000      960K     C:\windows\syswow64\RPCRT4.dll
0x76280000      384K     C:\windows\system32\IMM32.DLL
0x762e0000      816K     C:\windows\syswow64\MSCTF.dll
0x763e0000      280K     C:\windows\syswow64\KERNELBASE.dll
0x76430000      1024K    C:\windows\syswow64\USER32.dll
0x76530000      40K      C:\windows\syswow64\LPK.dll
0x76540000      688K     C:\windows\syswow64\msvcrt.dll
0x76870000      20K      C:\windows\syswow64\PSAPI.DLL
0x76880000      348K     C:\windows\syswow64\SHLWAPI.dll
0x768e0000      576K     C:\windows\syswow64\GDI32.dll
0x76b50000      100K     C:\windows\SysWOW64\sechost.dll
0x77140000      24K      C:\windows\syswow64\NSI.dll
0x77170000      1536K    C:\windows\SysWOW64\ntdll.dll
```

Object Histogram

Object histograms can be collected using the utilities available in HSDB and CLHSDB. A standalone tool is also available that can be used to dump object histograms from the target VM:

```
D:\ >java -classpath %JAVA_HOME%\lib\sa-jdi.jar
sun.jvm.hotspot.tools.ObjectHistogram 6468
Attaching to process ID 6468, please wait...
Debugger attached successfully.
Client compiler detected.
JVM version is 24.0-b56
Iterating over heap. This may take a while...
Object Histogram:

num       #instances      #bytes  Class description
--------------------------------------------------------------------------
1:            5659        546080  * ConstMethodKlass
2:            5659        455376  * MethodKlass
3:             385        221880  * ConstantPoolKlass
4:             385        154496  * InstanceKlassKlass
5:            1687        149824  char[]
6:             353        139264  * ConstantPoolCacheKlass
7:             477        122920  byte[]
8:             445         54320  java.lang.Class
9:             644         37600  * System ObjArray
10:            583         37008  short[]
11:           1364         32736  java.lang.String
12:            377         21064  int[]
13:             43         14104  * ObjArrayKlassKlass
14:            328         13544  java.lang.Object[]
15:            120          7680  java.lang.reflect.Field
16:             30          3232  java.util.HashMap$Entry[]
17:            125          3000  java.util.HashMap$Entry
18:            118          2832  java.util.Hashtable$Entry
19:              8          2624  * TypeArrayKlassKlass
20:             73          2472  java.lang.String[]
21:             12          1680  java.util.Hashtable$Entry[]
22:             96          1536  java.lang.StringBuilder
23:             38          1520  sun.util.locale.LocaleObjectCache$CacheEntry
.........
.......
228:             1             8  java.lang.Terminator$1
229:             1             8  java.security.ProtectionDomain$1
230:             1             8  sun.net.www.protocol.file.Handler
Total :      20102       2059376
Heap traversal took 0.153 seconds.
```

Structured Object Query Language—SOQL

This tool provides a shell-like command-line interface for executing SOQL queries. SOQL is an SQL-like language that can be used to query the Java heap:

```
java -classpath %JAVA_HOME%\lib\sa-jdi.jar
sun.jvm.hotspot.tools.soql.SOQL 5684
Attaching to process ID 5684, please wait...
Debugger attached successfully.
Client compiler detected.
JVM version is 24.0-b56
soql> select mirror(t) from java.lang.Thread t
> go
Thread[main,5,main]
Thread[Signal Dispatcher,9,system]
Thread[Attach Listener,5,system]
Thread[C1 CompilerThread0,9,system]
Thread[Service Thread,9,system]
```

jhat also provides an interface to use this language. Good documentation on this language is available in the jhat tool. That help documentation can also be accessed from here: https://blogs.oracle.com/poonam/entry/object_query_language_help.

ClassDump

Using this tool, we can dump the loaded classes from the target VM. It is possible to dump a single class or multiple classes from the selected packages. A few system properties are available that can be set to specify the name of the class that we want to dump or the list of packages from which we want to dump the classes. These are listed in Table 4.1.

Table 4.1 ClassDump Properties

System Property	Remarks
-Dsun.jvm.hotspot.tools.jcore.filter=<name of class>	Set the name of the class to be dumped.
-Dsun.jvm.hotspot.tools.jcore.PackageNameFilter.pkgList=<list of packages>	Specify a comma-separated list of packages whose classes we want to dump.
-Dsun.jvm.hotspot.tools.jcore.outputDir=<output directory>	Set the output directory where the classes should be dumped.

Here is how we can attach the ClassDump utility to a running process and dump the loaded classes in a folder specified using the -Dsun.jvm.hotspot.tools. jcore.outputDir property:

```
java -classpath $JAVA_HOME/lib/sa-jdi.jar
-Dsun.jvm.hotspot.tools.jcore.outputDir=
classes sun.jvm.hotspot.tools.jcore.ClassDump 2402
Attaching to process ID 2402, please wait...
Debugger attached successfully.
Server compiler detected.
JVM version is 24.0-b56

myserver 20 % ls classes
./                   ../                      TestClass.class   java/           sun/
```

As we can see, the ClassDump utility has dumped the classes loaded in the process in the classes/ folder. Similarly, this tool can attach to a core file or to a remote debug server and dump the classes loaded in the target VM.

DumpJFR

DumpJFR is an SA-based tool that can be used to extract Java Flight Recorder (JFR) information from the core files and live HotSpot processes.

Java Flight Recorder and Mission Control tools are shipped with the JDK since JDK 7u40. As we know, the Java Flight Recorder is a tool for collecting diagnostic and profiling data about a running Java application. It is integrated into the JVM, and its usage causes almost no performance overhead. Java Mission Control can be used to analyze the data collected by the Java Flight Recorder.

DumpJFR provides the capability to extract the JFR data from the core files of crashes, or hung Java processes, which otherwise is not possible to access. This tool is shipped with the JDK since JDK 8u60.

DumpJFR tool sources are present under hotspot/src/closed/agent/ in the repository. During the build process of HotSpot sources, DumpJFR class files get included into sa-jdi.jar when the closed part of the HotSpot repository gets built.

Please note that Java Flight Recorder and Mission Control, and hence this tool, require a commercial license for use in production.

This is how we can attach DumpJFR to a live process and dump the JFR data into a recording file:

```
java -cp $JAVA_HOME/lib/sa-jdi.jar sun.jvm.hotspot.tools.DumpJFR <pid>
```

This attaches DumpJFR to a core file to extract the Java Flight Recorder information:

```
java -cp $JAVA_HOME/lib/sa-jdi.jar sun.jvm.hotspot.tools.DumpJFR
<java> <core>
```

The DumpJFR tool dumps the JFR data to a file called recording.jfr in the current working folder. This recording file can be analyzed using Java Mission Control.

JSDB

JavaScript Debugger provides a JavaScript interface to the SA. It is a command-line JavaScript shell based on Mozilla's Rhino JavaScript Engine.

```
java -classpath %JAVA_HOME%\lib\sa-jdi.jar
sun.jvm.hotspot.tools.soql.JSDB 5684
Attaching to process ID 5684, please wait...
Debugger attached successfully.
Client compiler detected.
JVM version is 24.0-b56
jsdb>
```

More details on this utility can be found in the open-source HotSpot repository in the file hotspot/agent/doc/jsdb.html.

Core Dump or Crash Dump Files

We have been talking about the core files on Unix systems and the crash dump files on Windows systems. Here is a quick briefing on what these dump files are.

A core or crash dump file is a binary file that consists of the state of a running program at a specific time. A core file is generally created when a program terminates unexpectedly, due to a violation of the operating system's or hardware's protection mechanisms. The operating system kills the program and creates a core file that programmers can later use to figure out what went wrong. It contains a detailed description of the state that the program was in when it died.

It is also possible to create a core/crash dump file at will from a running (non-crashing) program. On Solaris/Linux, there is a tool called gcore that can dump the state of a running or hung process into a core file. On Windows, we can use WinDbg, userdump, or ADPlus to collect the crash dump files.

Core dump files are very useful for diagnosing and debugging problems in Java programs whenever it is difficult to debug the live processes.

Debugging Transported Core Files

Sometimes a core file is created on one system (core host) and we need to debug it on some other system (debugger host). Native debuggers (dbx, gdb) as well as the SA are not always able to open the transported core files successfully, the reason being a mismatch in the kernel and shared libraries between the system where the core was produced and the one where we are trying to debug it. Debuggers may face problems due to the mismatch of the following two types of libraries:

- The shared libraries used by the program on the core host may not be the same as those on the debugger host. So we need to make the original libraries from the core host available on the debugger system.

- Debuggers use the system libraries (e.g., libraries in /usr/lib, /lib64, etc.) to understand the implementation details of the runtime linker and the threads library on the system. To load the core files successfully we also need to get the system libraries from the core host and make them available on the debugger host.

If the core file was produced from a crash and a crash log hs_err file was also generated, we can get the list of the shared libraries (system and program) loaded by the process from the hs_err log file.

Shared Library Problems with the SA

When using SA with transported core files, we may get failures related to rtld_db or libthread_db mismatch, or SA may throw errors that some HotSpot symbol is missing in the target process. For example, in the following we are trying to open a core file with SA on a Linux/x64 machine transported from another Linux/x64 system:

```
-bash-3.2$ $JAVA_HOME/bin/java -classpath $JAVA_HOME/lib/sa-jdi.jar
 sun.jvm.hotspot.CLHSDB $JAVA_HOME/bin/java core.16963
Opening core file, please wait...
Unable to open core file
core.16963:

Doesn't appear to be a HotSpot VM (could not find symbol "gHotSpotVMTypes"
in remote process)
sun.jvm.hotspot.debugger.DebuggerException: Doesn't appear to be a HotSpot
VM (could not find symbol "gHotSpotVMTypes" in remote process)
        at sun.jvm.hotspot.HotSpotAgent.setupVM(HotSpotAgent.java:405)
        at sun.jvm.hotspot.HotSpotAgent.go(HotSpotAgent.java:314)
        at sun.jvm.hotspot.HotSpotAgent.attach(HotSpotAgent.java:173)
        at sun.jvm.hotspot.CLHSDB.attachDebugger(CLHSDB.java:188)
        at sun.jvm.hotspot.CLHSDB.run(CLHSDB.java:55)
        at sun.jvm.hotspot.CLHSDB.main(CLHSDB.java:35)
hsdb> Input stream closed.
```

SA is not able to open this transported core file.

Eliminate Shared Library Problems

So, how do we fix shared library problems encountered when opening transported core files with the SA? Here is what we can do to eliminate these problems:

1. Copy all the libraries used by the program from the core host to the debugger host, say, to a folder /space/corelibs/. Note that the libraries can be copied either directly under /space/corelibs/ or to a full directory path under /space/corelibs/. For example, /local/java/jre/lib/sparc/server/libjvm.so from the core host can be copied directly either under /space/corelibs/ or under /space/corelibs/local/java/ jre/lib/sparc/server/ on the debugger host. Similarly, /usr/lib/libthread_db.so from the core host can be copied either to /space/corelibs/ or to /space/corelibs/ usr/lib/ on the debugger host.

   The list of required library files can be obtained either from the hs_err log file under the section "Dynamic Libraries" or by using the native debuggers such as gdb, dbx, and WinDbg.

2. Then set the SA environment variable SA_ALTROOT to the folder containing the shared libraries on the debugger host, that is, setenv SA_ALTROOT /space/ corelibs/.

Now, for the core file core.16963 that we tried to open in the previous section, we copied all the required libraries from the core host to the system where we want to open the core with SA and then set the environment variable SA_ALTROOT:

```
-bash-3.2$ export SA_ALTROOT=/space/corelibs/
-bash-3.2$ $JAVA_HOME/bin/java -classpath $JAVA_HOME/lib/sa-jdi.jar
sun.jvm.hotspot.CLHSDB $JAVA_HOME/bin/java core.16963
Opening core file, please wait...
hsdb> universe
Heap Parameters:
ParallelScavengeHeap [ PSYoungGen [ eden =
[0x00000000eaa00000,0x00000000eaa00000,0x00000000faa80000] , from =
[0x00000000faa80000,0x00000000fb64975
0,0x00000000fd540000] , to =
[0x00000000fd540000,0x00000000fd540000,0x0000000100000000] ] PSOldGen [
[0x00000000bfe00000,0x00000000bfe12010,0x00000
000eaa00000] ] PSPermGen [
[0x00000000bac00000,0x00000000bc0942c0,0x00000000bc200000] ] ]
hsdb>
```

With SA_ALTROOT, SA picks up the required libraries from /space/corelibs/ and thus can open the core file successfully.

System Properties for the Serviceability Agent

There are some system properties that can be used to define the runtime behavior of the SA tools. These are shown in Table 4.2.

Table 4.2 Serviceability Agent System Properties

System Property	Remarks	Applicable Platforms
`sun.jvm.hotspot.runtime.VM.disableVersionCheck`	Disable the version check of the SA tools against the HotSpot version being analyzed.	All
`sun.jvm.hotspot.debugger.useProcDebugger` (Applicable only in JDK 6 and its updates)	Tell SA to use the `/proc` interface for reading bits from core/process. The other native interface uses `dbx` as the back end to attach to process/core and read data. This property is applicable only to SA in JDK 6 and is not present in JDK 7. ProcDebugger is the default in JDK 7 SA.	Solaris
`sun.jvm.hotspot.debugger.useWindbgDebugger` (Applicable only in JDK 6 and its updates)	Tell SA to use the Windows Debugger Engine (dbgeng.dll) interface for reading bits from processes and crash dump files. The other interface works only for live processes and talks to the Free Windows Debug Server (FwDbgSrv) over a socket to implement attach/detach and read bits from process memory. This property is applicable only to SA in JDK 6 and is not present in JDK 7. WinDbg Debugger is the default native interface in JDK 7.	Windows
`sun.jvm.hotspot.debugger.windbg.imagePath`	Set the path where SA on Windows should look for .exe and .dll files.	Windows
`sun.jvm.hotspot.debugger.windbg.symbolPath`	Set the path where SA on Windows should look for .pdb and .dbg symbol files.	Windows
`sun.jvm.hotspot.debugger.windbg.disableNativeLookup`	Specify if SA on Windows should parse the `DLL` symbol table in the Java code or use WinDbg's native lookup facility. By default, SA uses native lookup so that it can take advantage of .pdb files, if available.	Windows

Continued

System Property	Remarks	Applicable Platforms
`sun.jvm.hotspot.loadLibrary.DEBUG`	Enable printing of debug messages about native library loading on the Windows platform.	Windows
`sun.jvm.hotspot.tools.jcore.filter`	Specify the name of the class that we want to dump from the target VM.	All
`sun.jvm.hotspot.tools.jcore.PackageNameFilter.pkgList`	Specify a comma-separated package list whose classes we want to dump from the target VM.	All
`sun.jvm.hotspot.tools.jcore.outputDir`	Specify the output directory where we want to dump the class(es) from the target VM.	All

Environment Variables for the Serviceability Agent

There are some environment variables that can be set to define the runtime behavior of the SA tools. These are shown in Table 4.3.

Table 4.3 Serviceability Agent Environment Variables

Environment Variable	Remarks	Applicable Platforms
`SA_ALTROOT`	Set the directory location where SA should look for the shared libraries when opening transported core files on the debugger host.	Solaris and Linux
`LIBSAPROC_DEBUG`	Enable printing of debug messages from the SA native binary libsaproc.so to standard error.	Solaris and Linux
	SA on Solaris uses the libproc.so library. This library also prints debug messages with environment variable `LIBPROC_DEBUG`. Setting `LIBSAPROC_DEBUG` also sets the `LIBPROC_DEBUG` variable.	
`SA_IGNORE_THREADDB`	When opening transported core files, if we are getting `libthread_db`-related failures due to mismatch of libraries, we can set this environment variable. With this set, SA ignores `libthread_db` failure and can open the core files successfully, but we will not get any thread-related information.	Solaris and Linux

JDI Implementation

The SA binary sa-jdi.jar also has an implementation of the Java Debug Interface (JDI) that makes it possible for any JDI client (e.g., JDB) to attach to the core files and also Java processes using the JDI Connectors provided by this implementation.

The VM object returned by the `attach()` method of these connectors is read-only. This means that the obtained VM object cannot be modified. So, JDI clients using these connectors should not call any JDI methods that are defined to throw a `VMCannotBeModifiedException`.

SA Core Attaching Connector

This connector can be used by a debugger application to debug a core file. It allows multiple debugging sessions on the same core file. It is uniquely identified by the name `sun.jvm.hotspot.jdi.SACoreAttachingConnector` and can be used as in the following:

```
$JAVA_HOME/bin/jdb
-J-Xbootclasspath/a:$JAVA_HOME/lib/sa-jdi.jar:$JAVA_HOME/lib/tools.jar
-connect sun.jvm.hotspot.jdi.SACoreAttachingConnector:core=
${CORE_FILE},javaExecutable=${EXEC_FILE}
```

SAPID Attaching Connector

This connector can be used by a debugger application to debug a process. The process to be debugged need not have been started in the debug mode (i.e., with `-agentlib:jdwp` or `-Xrunjdwp`), and it is permissible for the process to be hung. Using this connector, the debugger gets a read-only view of the process, and the VM object obtained after attaching to the process cannot be modified.

The process is suspended when this connector attaches and is resumed when the connector detaches. More than one SAPID Attaching Connector cannot attach to a single process simultaneously. This connector is uniquely identified by the name `sun.jvm.hotspot.jdi.SAPIDAttachingConnector`.

Debuggers can use this connector as in the following to connect to and debug a process:

```
$JAVA_HOME/bin/jdb
-J-Xbootclasspath/a:$JAVA_HOME/lib/sa-jdi.jar:$JAVA_HOME/lib/tools.jar
-connect sun.jvm.hotspot.jdi.SAPIDAttachingConnector:pid=2402
```

SA Debug Server Attaching Connector

This connector can be used by a debugger application to debug a process or core file on a machine other than the machine on which the debugger is running. This connector uses Remote Method Invocation (RMI) to communicate with a debug server running on the remote machine. Before the `attach()` method on this connector is called, the debug server must be started on the remote machine and told what process or core file is to be debugged. The following needs to be done on the remote machine:

1. Start the RMI registry with sa-jdi.jar in the classpath:

```
${JAVA_HOME}/bin/rmiregistry
-J-Xbootclasspath/p:${JAVA_HOME}/lib/sa-jdi.jar
```

This command creates and starts a remote object registry. An optional port number may be specified as the the port number at which the registry should be started. If no optional port number is specified, the registry is started on port 1099.

2. Start the debug server on the remote machine, specifying the process or core file to be debugged:

```
${JAVA_HOME}/bin/java -classpath ${JAVA_HOME}/lib/sa-jdi.jar
sun.jvm.hotspot.jdi.SADebugServer <pid> [uniqueID]
```

or

```
${JAVA_HOME}/bin/java -classpath ${JAVA_HOME}/lib/sa-jdi.jar
sun.jvm.hotspot.jdi.SADebugServer
<pathname to the java executable that produced the core file>
<pathname of the core file to debug> [uniqueID]
```

SA Debug Server starts the RMI registry at port 1099 if the registry is not already running.

An alternative to these two steps is to use the `jsadebugd` utility that is shipped with the JDK to start the RMI registry and the debug server on the remote machine.

`uniqueID` is an optional string. If more than one debug server is to run at the same time on the same machine, each must have a different `uniqueID` string.

Extending Serviceability Agent Tools

The Serviceability Agent APIs provide a class `sun.jvm.hotspot.tools.Tool` which can be extended to write our own troubleshooting tools.

Here is a simple tool extending the `sun.jvm.hotspot.tools.Tool` class that prints the system properties of the target VM. This tool is part of the sa-jdi.jar file:

```java
package sun.jvm.hotspot.tools;

import java.io.PrintStream;
import java.util.*;
import sun.jvm.hotspot.runtime.*;

public class SysPropsDumper extends Tool {

    public void run() {
        Properties sysProps = VM.getVM().getSystemProperties();
        PrintStream out = System.out;
        if (sysProps != null) {
            Enumeration keys = sysProps.keys();
            while (keys.hasMoreElements()) {
                Object key = keys.nextElement();
                out.print(key);
                out.print(" = ");
                out.println(sysProps.get(key));
            }
        } else {
            out.println("System Properties info not available!");
        }
    }

    public static void main(String[] args) {
        SysPropsDumper pd = new SysPropsDumper();
        pd.start(args);
        pd.stop();
    }
}
```

To write our own tool, we need to extend it from the `Tool` class and implement the `run()` method where we add the main functionality of the tool. In the preceding example, using the VM class we obtain the system properties and then print those properties to the standard output.

Let's compile and run this tool against a running process and see what the output looks like:

```
D:\>javac -classpath %JAVA_HOME%\lib\sa-jdi.jar
sun/jvm/hotspot/tools/SysPropsDumper.java
D:\>java -classpath %JAVA_HOME%\lib\sa-jdi.jar
```

Continued

```
sun.jvm.hotspot.tools.SysPropsDumper 5880
Attaching to process ID 5880, please wait...
Debugger attached successfully.
Client compiler detected.
JVM version is 24.0-b56
java.runtime.name = Java(TM) SE Runtime Environment
java.vm.version = 24.0-b56
sun.boot.library.path = D:\Java\7u40\jre\bin
java.vendor.url = http://java.oracle.com/
java.vm.vendor = Oracle Corporation
path.separator = ;
file.encoding.pkg = sun.io
java.vm.name = Java HotSpot(TM) Client VM
sun.os.patch.level = Service Pack 1
sun.java.launcher = SUN_STANDARD
user.script =
user.country = US
user.dir = D:\tests
java.vm.specification.name = Java Virtual Machine Specification
java.runtime.version = 1.7.0_40-b43
java.awt.graphicsenv = sun.awt.Win32GraphicsEnvironment
os.arch = x86
java.endorsed.dirs = D:\Java\7u40\jre\lib\endorsed
line.separator =

java.io.tmpdir = C:\Users\pobajaj\AppData\Local\Temp\
java.vm.specification.vendor = Oracle Corporation
user.variant =
os.name = Windows 7
sun.jnu.encoding = Cp1252
java.library.path = D:\Java\7u40\bin;C:\windows\Sun\Java\bin;C:\windows\
system32;C:\windows;C:\Java\7u40\bin;C:\windows\system32;C:\windows;C:
\windows\System32\Wbem;C:\windows\System32\WindowsPowerShell\v1.0\;C:\Program
Files (x86)\Microsoft SQL Server\100\Tools\Binn\;C:\Program Files\Micros
oft SQL Server\100\Tools\Binn\;C:\Program Files\Microsoft SQL Server\100\
DTS\Binn\;D:\Program Files\Perforce;.
java.specification.name = Java Platform API Specification
java.class.version = 51.0
sun.management.compiler = HotSpot Client Compiler
os.version = 6.1
user.home = C:\Users\pobajaj
user.timezone =
java.awt.printerjob = sun.awt.windows.WPrinterJob
file.encoding = Cp1252
java.specification.version = 1.7
user.name = pobajaj
java.class.path = .
java.vm.specification.version = 1.7
sun.arch.data.model = 32
sun.java.command = TestClass
java.home = D:\Java\7u40\jre
user.language = en
java.specification.vendor = Oracle Corporation
awt.toolkit = sun.awt.windows.WToolkit
```

```
java.vm.info = mixed mode, sharing
java.version = 1.7.0_40
java.ext.dirs = D:\Java\7u40\jre\lib\ext;C:\windows\Sun\Java\lib\ext
sun.boot.class.path = D:\Java\7u40\jre\lib\resources.jar;D:\Java\7u40\jre\
lib\rt.jar;D:\Java\7u40\jre\lib\sunrsasign.jar;D:\Java\7u40\jre\lib\jsse
.jar;D:\Java\7u40\jre\lib\jce.jar;D:\Java\7u40\jre\lib\charsets.jar;D:\
Java\7u40\jre\lib\jfr.jar;D:\Java\7u40\jre\classes
java.vendor = Oracle Corporation
file.separator =
java.vendor.url.bug = http://bugreport.sun.com/bugreport/
sun.io.unicode.encoding = UnicodeLittle
sun.cpu.endian = little
sun.desktop = windows
sun.cpu.isalist = pentium_pro+mmx pentium_pro pentium+mmx pentium i486
i386 i86
```

The SA code is located under the <hotspot-repo>/agent/src/ folder, and the implementation of a few tools that get bundled with sa-jdi.jar exists under sun/jvm/hotspot/tools/ under that folder.

The JavaDoc API for these classes is available for download from http://docs.oracle.com/javase/8/docs/serviceabilityagent/.

Serviceability Agent Plugin for VisualVM

Before we delve into the details on the Serviceability Agent Plugin for Java VisualVM (VisualVM), let's first talk briefly about VisualVM.

VisualVM is a visual tool for troubleshooting, monitoring, and observing Java applications. It is positioned as an all-in-one monitoring and troubleshooting tool for Java applications. Most of the standalone tools shipped with the JDK such as jstack, jmap, and so on are also available in VisualVM. Starting with JDK 6u7, VisualVM is also shipped with the JDK and can be launched using the command jvisualvm. Figure 4.36 shows an example of what VisualVM looks like when it has been launched.

One great thing about VisualVM is that it is possible to extend it using plugins. One can write plugins for VisualVM using its APIs and develop plugins for others to use. The plugins then can be made available in the VisualVM Plugins Center.

Serviceability Agent Plugin for VisualVM is a VisualVM plugin that brings key features of SA to VisualVM. This plugin provides the ability to look at the VM representation of Java objects in the heap, Java threads in the application, and compiled/interpreted code of methods and to find references for a given address in the Java heap, all from within the VisualVM GUI.

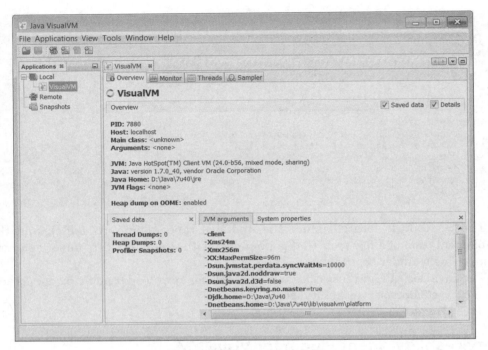

Figure 4.36 Java VisualVM

How to Install the SA-Plugin in VisualVM

VisualVM plugins are available at the VisualVM Plugins Center. The latest VisualVM Plugins Center is at http://visualvm.java.net/pluginscenters.html. To install the SA-Plugin in VisualVM, click on Tools > Plugins. This will bring up the Plugins dialog box. Click on the Available Plugins tab, select SAPlugin from the list, and then click Install. This will install the SA-Plugin in your VisualVM installation.

How to Use the SA-Plugin

Let's take a look how we can use the SA-Plugin to explore a running process or a core file.

To explore a live process with SA-Plugin, run the process with a JDK that is shipped along with the SA binaries. Open this process in VisualVM. When SA-Plugin is installed in VisualVM, the SAPlugin tab appears in the Application view when the process is opened in VisualVM. Now, click Attach to Process in the SAPlugin tab; this will attach SA to the running process, and the process will be paused at that point in time. Now we can explore the snapshot of the process. We can look at its Java threads, inspect the Java objects, look at the bytecodes/compiled code of methods, and so on.

After we are done, we can detach the process from the SA by clicking the Detach from Process button. The process will resume.

Opening and diagnosing core files is similar to exploring processes with SA-Plugin. First we need to open the core file in VisualVM and then attach to that core from the SA Plugin view. As in the case of a process, we can explore objects in the Java heap, look at thread objects, search for values in the Java heap, and look at the compiled code of methods from the core file. SA-Plugin's capability of exploring the core files helps a great deal in the postmortem of dead processes.

SA-Plugin Utilities

This plugin makes some of the Serviceability Agent utilities available in the VisualVM in four panels described in the following sections.

Java Threads/Java Stack Trace

This panel, shown in Figure 4.37, shows all the Java threads in the attached process or core file. Double-clicking on any thread or clicking on the Open Inspector icon on the Java Threads panel shows internal details of the thread object in another Oop

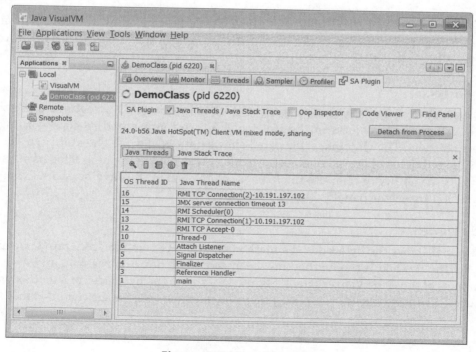

Figure 4.37 Java Threads

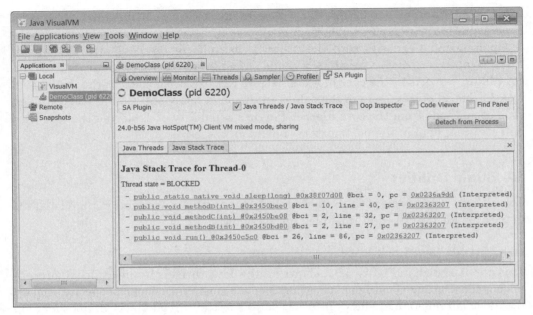

Figure 4.38 Java Stack Trace

Inspector panel. And clicking on the Show Stack Trace icon on the Java Threads panel shows the stack trace of the thread. An example of the Show Stack Trace panel is shown in Figure 4.38.

Oop Inspector

We can inspect the Java objects as well as the VM internal C++ structures using this panel. All the Java objects in the HotSpot VM are represented as oops—ordinary object pointers. The Oop Inspector panel shows details of oops. The ability to see all the internal fields of any Java object provides great debugging help. This panel also provides the ability to compute the liveness of any oop in the Java heap. An example of the Oop Inspector panel is shown in Figure 4.39.

Code Viewer

This panel shows the bytecodes of a method and the JIT compiler-generated machine code of the method if the method has been compiled. See Figures 4.40 and 4.41 for examples of the Code Viewer panel. Figure 4.40 shows the bytecodes of a method, and Figure 4.41 shows the JIT compiler-generated machine code for the compiled method.

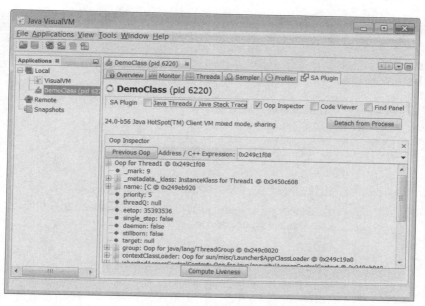

Figure 4.39 Oop Inspector

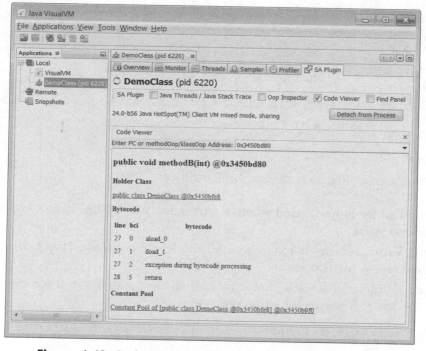

Figure 4.40 Code Viewer showing bytecodes of a method

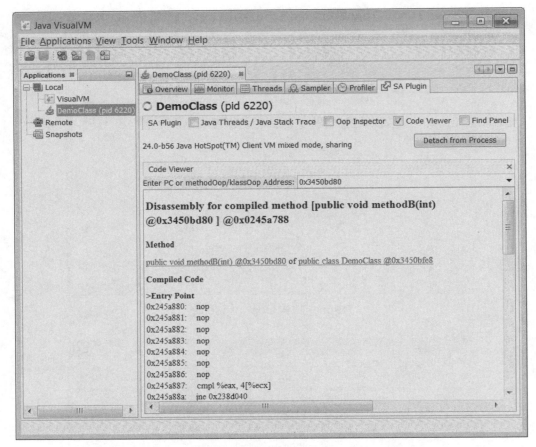

Figure 4.41 Code Viewer showing compiled code

Find Panel

This panel, seen in Figure 4.42, has three utilities:

- Find Pointer helps us find where a particular address lies in the Java process address space.
- Find Value in Heap helps us find all the locations in the Java heap where a particular value is present.
- Find Value in CodeCache helps us find all the locations in the compiler code cache where a particular value is present.

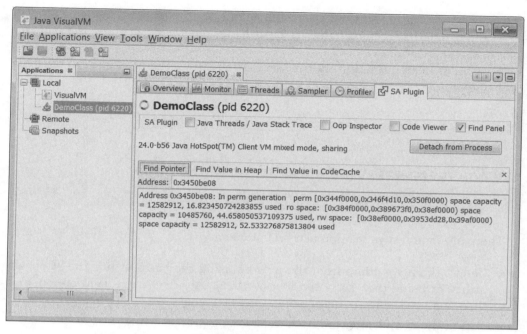

Figure 4.42 Find panel

Troubleshooting Problems Using the SA

In the previous sections we looked at what the SA is and how it works. In this section we will talk a bit about the real-world problems of Java applications and then see in detail how SA can help us get to the root of these issues.

A Java application can face multiple problems: slowness, huge memory consumption, unexpected behavior of the program, and even crashes. SA tools can greatly help in figuring out the root cause of these and also help improve the performance of applications.

Diagnosing `OutOfMemoryError`

`java.lang.OutOfMemoryError` is thrown when there is insufficient space to allocate new objects in the Java heap or in the permanent generation space or metaspace. (Please note that in JDK 8, permanent generation space has been removed in favor of the metaspace.) At that point, the garbage collector cannot make any more space available and the heap cannot be expanded further.

The possible reasons for this error could be that the footprint of the application is large and cannot be accommodated in the specified Java heap, or there is a memory leak in the application.

Here is a Java program that throws `java.lang.OutOfMemoryError` in the Java heap space:

```
D:\tests>java MemoryError
Exception in thread "main" java.lang.OutOfMemoryError: Java heap space
        at java.util.Vector.<init>(Vector.java:131)
        at java.util.Vector.<init>(Vector.java:144)
        at java.util.Vector.<init>(Vector.java:153)
        at Employee.<init>(MemoryError.java:42)
        at MemoryError.main(MemoryError.java:14)
```

There are many ways to approach this problem:

- Collect the heap dump from the process using the `jmap` utility, the JConsole utility, or using the `-XX:+HeapDumpOnOutOfMemoryError` JVM option, and then analyze the heap dump using `jhat` or VisualVM.
- Collect the heap histogram from the running process using the SA tools.
- Collect the core or crash dump file at the occurrence of `OutOfMemoryError` using the `-XX:OnOutOfMemoryError` option, and then obtain the heap histogram from that core/crash dump file using the SA tools.

Since our program does not run for long and does not give us enough time to attach any tool to the running process, we run the process with `-XX:OnOutOfMemoryError` to produce a crash dump file when the `OutOfMemoryError` occurs. We are running this program on a Windows machine.

```
D:\tests>java -XX:OnOutOfMemoryError="D:\Tools\userdump8.1\x64\userdump
%p" MemoryError
#
# java.lang.OutOfMemoryError: Java heap space
# -XX:OnOutOfMemoryError="D:\Tools\userdump8.1\x64\userdump %p"
#   Executing "D:\Tools\userdump8.1\x64\userdump 4768"...
User Mode Process Dumper (Version 8.1.2929.5)
Copyright (c) Microsoft Corp. All rights reserved.
Dumping process 4768 (java.exe) to
d:\tests\java.dmp...
The process was dumped successfully.
Exception in thread "main" java.lang.OutOfMemoryError: Java heap space
        at java.util.Vector.<init>(Vector.java:131)
        at java.util.Vector.<init>(Vector.java:144)
        at java.util.Vector.<init>(Vector.java:153)
        at Employee.<init>(MemoryError.java:42)
        at MemoryError.main(MemoryError.java:14)
```

To generate the core file on Solaris or Linux platforms, the program can be run as

```
java -XX:OnOutOfMemoryError="gcore %p" MemoryError
```

Now, let's open this crash dump file in the HSDB tool:

```
D:\tests>java -classpath %JAVA_HOME%\lib\sa-jdi.jar
sun.jvm.hotspot.HSDB %JAVA_HOME%\bin\java.exe java.dmp
```

Get the object histogram of the heap by clicking Tools > Object Histogram, as shown in Figure 4.43.

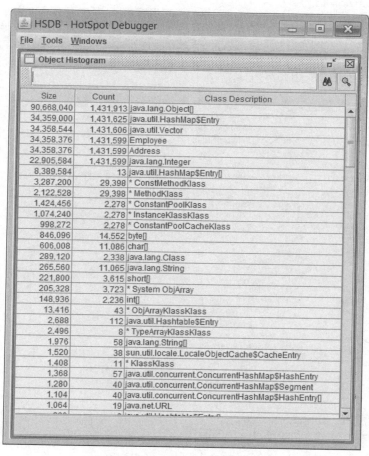

Figure 4.43 Object Histogram

This histogram shows that apart from the system classes, `Address` and `Employee` classes appear near the top of the histogram and occupy a lot of space in the heap. This tells us that the instances of these classes are the main culprits for the `OutOfMemoryError`.

In the Object Histogram utility, we can find out all the instances of a particular class that are present in the Java heap. To do this, there is an icon at the top right corner of the Object Histogram window. Let's find all the instances for the `Address` class. Figure 4.44 shows the Object Histogram window actively searching for all address instances.

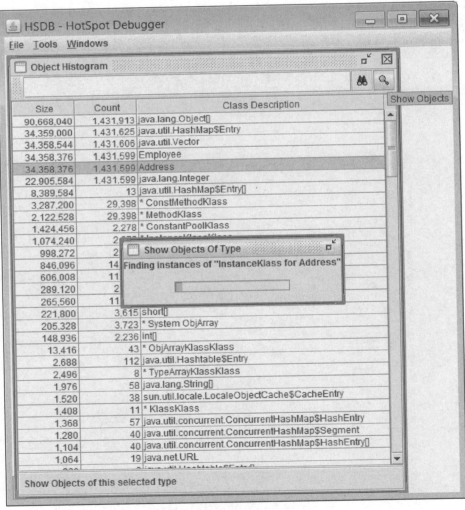

Figure 4.44 Show Objects

Finding all the instances may take some time as the tool has to traverse the whole heap. This will bring up the Show Objects of Type window for the `Address` class as shown in Figure 4.45.

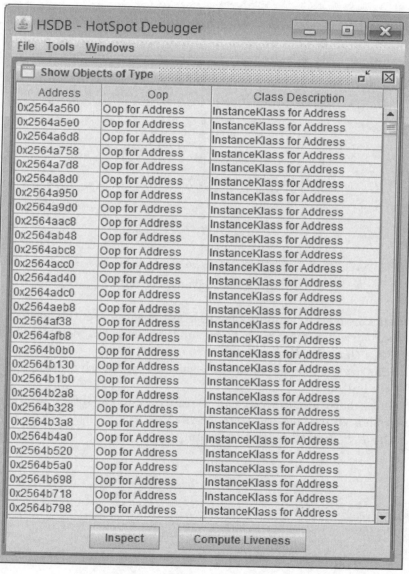

Figure 4.45 Show Objects of Type

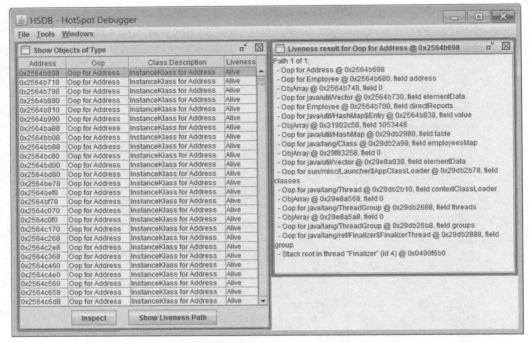

Figure 4.46 Liveness result

Now, by clicking on the Compute Liveness button we can get the liveness path (the reference path by which an instance is reachable from the GC roots) for the instances of the `Address` class. See Figure 4.46.

Then we can see the liveness path of the selected instance by clicking on the Show Liveness Path button.

The liveness path of the `Address` instance at 0x2564b698 shows that it is reachable from a Vector field `employeesList`.

Here is the Java code of the test program:

```
import java.util.*;
public class MemoryError{
    static Vector employeesList;
    public static void main(String arg[]) throws Exception{
        HashMap employeesMap = new HashMap();
        employeesList = new Vector();
        int i = 0;
        while(true){
            Employee emp1 =
                new Employee("Ram",
                    new Address("MG Road", "Bangalore", 123, "India"));
```

```
                Employee emp2 =
                    new Employee("Bob",
                        new Address("House No. 4", "SCA", 234, "USA"));
                Employee emp3 =
                    new Employee("John",
                        new Address("Church Street", "Bangalore",
                                569, "India"));
                employeesMap.put(new Integer(i++), emp1);
                employeesList.add(emp1);
                employeesMap.put(new Integer(i++), emp2);
                employeesList.add(emp2);
                employeesMap.put(new Integer(i++), emp3);
                employeesList.add(emp3);
                emp2.addReports(emp1);
                emp3.addReports(emp1);
                emp3.addReports(emp2);
            }
        }
    }
    class Employee{
        public String name;
        public Address address;
        public Vector directReports;
        public Employee(String nm, Address addr){
            name = nm;
            address = addr;
            directReports = new Vector();
        }
        public void addReports(Employee emp){
            directReports.add((Object)emp);
        }
    }
    class Address{
        public String addr;
        public String city;
        public int zip;
        public String country;
        public Address(String a, String ci, int z, String co){
            addr = a;
            city = ci;
            zip = z;
            city = co;
        }
    }
```

We can see that this Java code maintains records of employees along with their address details. The employee records are added to two collection objects: to a hash map and to a vector. Vector `employeesList` and hash map `employeeMap` hold references to the `Employee` and `Address` instances and thus prevent them from getting collected by the garbage collector. Therefore, these instances keep increasing in number in the Java heap.

This test program demonstrates a mistake that is commonly made in real applications. Often, applications inadvertently maintain multiple caches and collections of objects that are not required for the program logic, and that mistake increases the footprint of the process, thus leading to out-of-memory errors.

Please note that to demonstrate the problem and to produce the out-of-memory error, the employee records are added in a while loop in the test program, and that may not be the case in real-world applications.

We can also obtain the object histograms from the crash dump file using the Object Histogram standalone utility:

```
D:\tests>java -classpath %JAVA_HOME%\lib\sa-jdi.jar
sun.jvm.hotspot.tools.ObjectHistogram
%JAVA_HOME%\bin\java.exe java.dmp
Attaching to core java.dmp from executable D:\Java\7u40\bin\java.exe,
please wait...
Debugger attached successfully.
Client compiler detected.
JVM version is 24.0-b56
Iterating over heap. This may take a while...
Object Histogram:

num        #instances    #bytes  Class description
--------------------------------------------------------------------------
1:         1431913 90668040        java.lang.Object[]
2:         1431625 34359000        java.util.HashMap$Entry
3:         1431606 34358544        java.util.Vector
4:         1431599 34358376        Employee
5:         1431599 34358376        Address
6:         1431599 22905584        java.lang.Integer
7:         13      8389584 java.util.HashMap$Entry[]
8:         29398   3287200 * ConstMethodKlass
9:         29398   2122528 * MethodKlass
10:        2278    1424456 * ConstantPoolKlass
11:        2278    1074240 * InstanceKlassKlass
12:        2278    998272  * ConstantPoolCacheKlass
13:        14552   846096  byte[]
14:        11086   606008  char[]
.....

.....
166:       1       8       java.nio.Bits$1
167:       1       8       java.lang.Runtime
168:       1       8       java.security.ProtectionDomain$1
169:       1       8       java.lang.ref.Reference$Lock
170:       1       8       java.security.ProtectionDomain$3
Total :    8705181 270932344
Heap traversal took 125.427 seconds.
```

Diagnosing a Java-Level Deadlock

Let's look at a small Java program that gets locked up in a deadlock soon after the start of its execution:

```java
public class DeadLockTest extends Thread {
    public static Object lock1 = new Object();
    public static Object lock2 = new Object();
    private int index;
    public static void main(String[] a) {
        Thread t1 = new Thread0();
        Thread t2 = new Thread1();
        t1.start();
        t2.start();
    }

    private static class Thread0 extends Thread {
        public void run() {
            synchronized (lock1) {
                System.out.println("Thread 0: Holding lock 1...");
                try { Thread.sleep(10); }
                catch (InterruptedException e) {}
                System.out.println("Thread 0: Waiting for lock 2...");
                synchronized (lock2) {
                    System.out.println("Thread 0: Holding lock 1 & 2...");
                }
            }
        }
    }

    private static class Thread1 extends Thread {
        public void run() {
            synchronized (lock2) {
                System.out.println("Thread 1: Holding lock 2...");
                try { Thread.sleep(10); }
                catch (InterruptedException e) {}
                System.out.println("Thread 1: Waiting for lock 1...");
                synchronized (lock1) {
                    System.out.println("Thread 1: Holding lock 2 & 1...");
                }
            }
        }
    }
}
```

We start the execution of this program and then let it run for some time. The program enters deadlock soon after. Then we attach HSDB to the hung process. HSDB has a utility called Deadlock Detection that is available under the Tools menu. Upon launching the Deadlock Detection tool, we get the message window shown in Figure 4.47.

This shows that the program has one Java-level deadlock involving two threads—Thread-0 and Thread-1. Thread-0 is waiting to lock Monitor 0x00ef2aac, which is held by Thread-1, and Thread-1 is waiting to lock Monitor 0x00ef0f8c, which is already held by Thread-0; hence the deadlock.

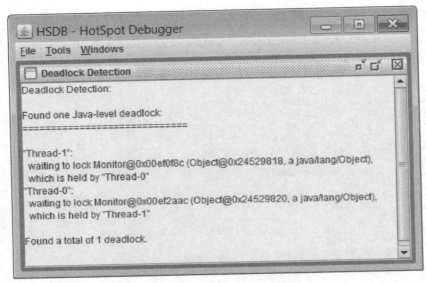

Figure 4.47 Deadlock Detection

To get more details on these monitors, we can use the Monitor Cache Dump utility. See Figure 4.48.

Sometimes, it is interesting to look at the state of the threads. We can do this by inspecting the thread object in the Oop Inspector utility. Let's take a look at the Thread-0 and Thread-1 thread objects in the Oop Inspector. Double-clicking on these threads in the Java Threads panel will bring up the Oop Inspector windows for these thread objects. Figure 4.49 shows the Oop Inspector for Thread-0, and Figure 4.50 shows the Oop Inspector window for Thread-1.

In these two snapshots, both threads have the thread status of 1025. Let's look at the code in Java HotSpot VM that computes the thread state of the Java thread from its `threadStatus` field:

```
public static Thread.State toThreadState(int threadStatus) {
    if ((threadStatus & JVMTI_THREAD_STATE_RUNNABLE) != 0) {
        return RUNNABLE;
    } else if ((threadStatus &
            JVMTI_THREAD_STATE_BLOCKED_ON_MONITOR_ENTER) != 0) {
        return BLOCKED;

private final static int
    JVMTI_THREAD_STATE_BLOCKED_ON_MONITOR_ENTER = 0x0400;
```

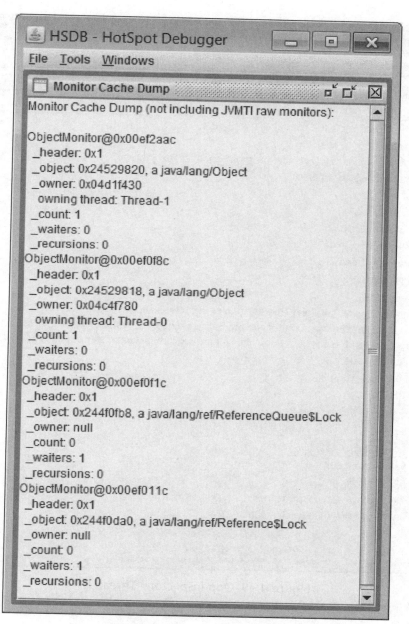

Figure 4.48 Monitor Cache Dump

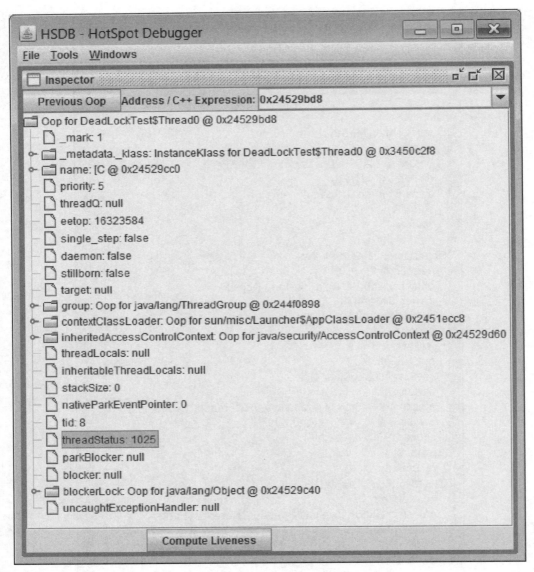

Figure 4.49 Oop Inspector—Thread-0

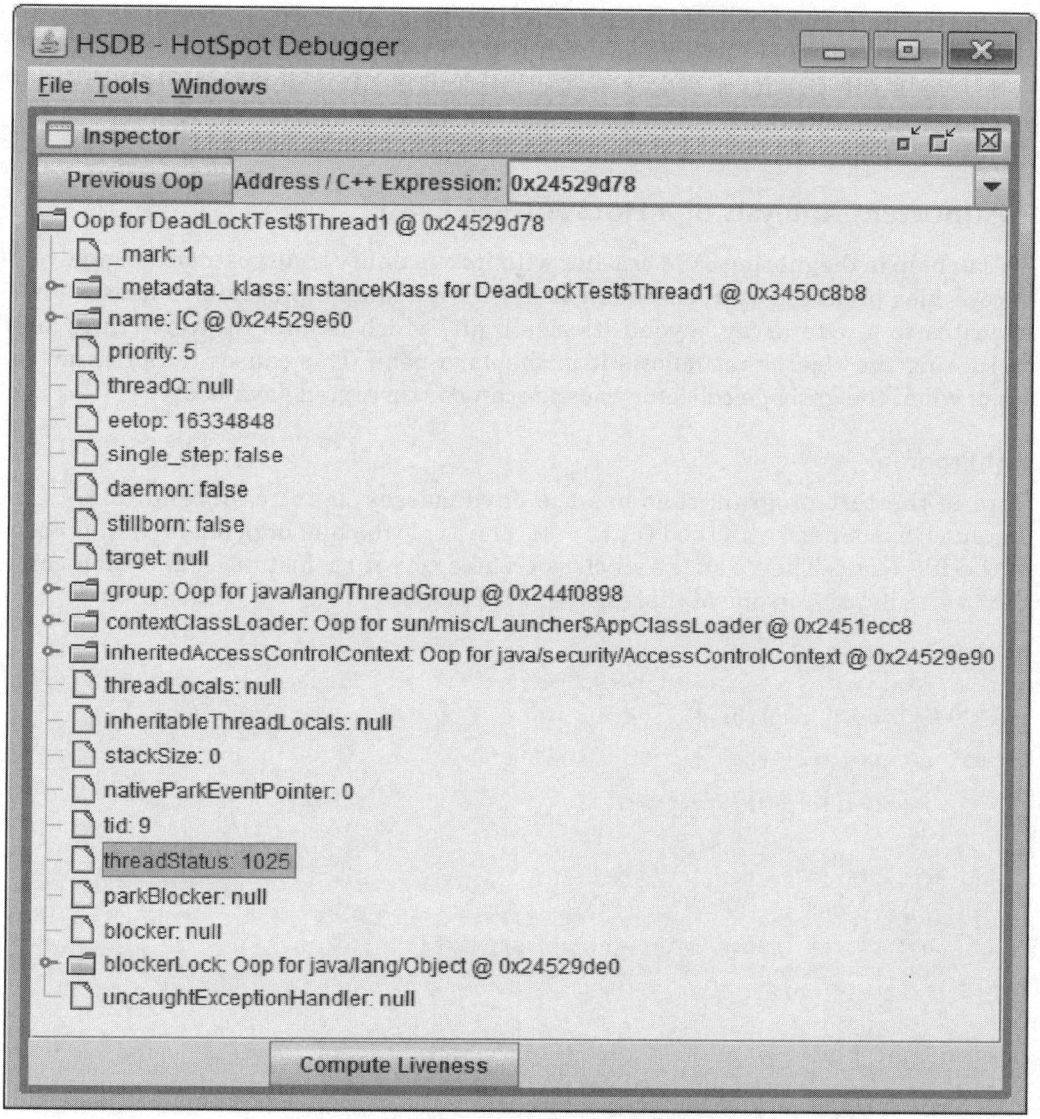

Figure 4.50 Oop Inspector—Thread-1

This computation would return the thread state as BLOCKED when the threadStatus is 1025. This means that both threads are in the BLOCKED state.

So, using the Deadlock Detection tool, we can easily nail down the Java-level deadlocks in applications.

Postmortem Analysis of a HotSpot VM Crash

SA can help in diagnosing JVM crashes with its capability to do postmortem analysis of core files produced with these crashes. I have a simple program that uses JNI. It writes to a byte array beyond its size limit, which results in overwriting and corrupting the object that follows it in the Java heap. This causes the program to crash when the garbage collector tries to scan the corrupted Java heap.

Test Program

Here is the test program that has the Java classes TestCrash and Object1. Object1 has a native method (nativeMethod()) which is implemented in C code in the file test.c. The TestCrash class creates Object1 instances and then calls nativeMethod() on one of these Object1 instances.

```java
import java.util.ArrayList;

public class TestCrash {
    static {
      System.loadLibrary("test");
    }

    ArrayList a2 = new ArrayList();
    ArrayList a3 = new ArrayList();

    public static void main(String[] args) {
        TestCrash t = new TestCrash();
        t.method1();
    }

    void method1() {
        /* Fill the heap with ArrayLists */
        ArrayList a1 = new ArrayList();
        for (int i=0; i<10000; i++) {
            Object1 obj = new Object1();
            a1.add(obj);
        }

        /* corrupt an object with native method*/
        ((Object1)a1.get(1)).nativeMethod();

        /* Invoke garbage collection */
        for (int p=0; p<10; p++) {
          System.gc();
```

```
        }
        try {
            Thread.sleep(1000);
        } catch (InterruptedException ex) {
        }
    }
}

class Object1 {
    byte[] array = {1, 2, 3};
    native void nativeMethod();
}
```

Here is the native part of the test case implementing method `nativeMethod()` using JNI. This source code is placed in a file named test.cpp following the JNI source file naming conventions.

```cpp
#include "test.h"
#include <stdlib.h>
#include <memory.h>

/*
 * Class:      Object1
 * Method:     nativeMethod
 * Signature:  ()V
 */

JNIEXPORT void JNICALL Java_Object1_nativeMethod
    (JNIEnv *env, jobject obj) {
        jclass cls = env->GetObjectClass(obj);
        jfieldID fldID = env->GetFieldID(cls, "array", "[B");
        jbyteArray arrayObject =
                    (jbyteArray)env->GetObjectField(obj, fldID);

        jbyte* array =
                (jbyte*)env->GetPrimitiveArrayCritical(arrayObject, 0);

        memcpy(array, "Hello Java.Hello
Java.Hello Java.Hello Java.Hello Java.Hello
Java.Hello Java.Hello Java.Hello Java.Hello Java.", 100);

        env->ReleasePrimitiveArrayCritical(arrayObject, array, 0);
        env->ExceptionDescribe();
        env->ExceptionClear();

}
```

Now, we need to compile this program on a Solaris machine with the following instructions:

```
export JAVA_HOME=/java/jdk1.7.0_40/
$JAVA_HOME/bin/javac TestCrash.java
CC -m32 -I$JAVA_HOME/include -I$JAVA_HOME/include/solaris -G
test.cpp -o libtest.so
```

and then execute it as shown here:

```
oracle@solaris_11X:/demo# java -Djava.library.path=. TestCrash
#
# A fatal error has been detected by the Java Runtime Environment:
#
#  SIGSEGV (0xb) at pc=0xfe20af22, pid=1860, tid=3
#
# JRE version: Java(TM) SE Runtime Environment (7.0_40-b43) (build
1.7.0_40-b43)
# Java VM: Java HotSpot(TM) Client VM (24.0-b56 mixed mode solaris-x86 )
# Problematic frame:
# V  [libjvm.so+0x20af22]  void
objArrayKlass::oop_follow_contents(oopDesc*)+0x1d2
#
# Core dump written. Default location: /demo/core or core.1860
#
# An error report file with more information is saved as:
# /demo/hs_err_pid1860.log
#
# If you would like to submit a bug report, please visit:
#   http://bugreport.sun.com/bugreport/crash.jsp
#
Abort (core dumped)
```

The program crashes with the following stack trace:

```
Stack: [0xe77c1000,0xe7841000],  sp=0xe783ff90,  free space=507k
Native frames: (J=compiled Java code, j=interpreted, Vv=VM code, C=native
code)
V  [libjvm.so+0x20af22]  void
objArrayKlass::oop_follow_contents(oopDesc*)+0x1d2
V  [libjvm.so+0x208f40]  void MarkSweep::follow_stack()+0xc0
V  [libjvm.so+0x1ef4a1]  void InterpreterFrameClosure::offset_do(int)+0x59
V  [libjvm.so+0x1ef3d1]  void
InterpreterOopMap::iterate_oop(OffsetClosure*)+0xd9
V  [libjvm.so+0x50af15]  void
frame::oops_do_
internal(OopClosure*,CodeBlobClosure*,RegisterMap*,bool)+0x901
V  [libjvm.so+0x9805c1]  void
JavaThread::oops_do(OopClosure*,CodeBlobClosure*)+0x1f5
V  [libjvm.so+0x98619a]  void
Threads::oops_do(OopClosure*,CodeBlobClosure*)+0x3a
V  [libjvm.so+0x8db11a]  void
SharedHeap::process_strong_
roots(bool,bool,SharedHeap::ScanningOption,OopClosure*,
CodeBlobClosure*,OopsInGenClosure*)+0xc2
```

```
V   [libjvm.so+0x5718db]   void
GenCollectedHeap::gen_process_strong_
roots(int,bool,bool,bool,SharedHeap::ScanningOption,
OopsInGenClosure*,bool,OopsInGenClosure*)+0x5b
V   [libjvm.so+0x574594]   void
GenMarkSweep::mark_sweep_phase1(int,bool)+0x88
V   [libjvm.so+0x573e5d]   void
GenMarkSweep::invoke_at_safepoint(int,ReferenceProcessor*,bool)+0x179
V   [libjvm.so+0x579d9e]   void
OneContigSpaceCardGeneration::collect(bool,bool,unsigned,bool)+0x8a
V   [libjvm.so+0x57116a]   void
GenCollectedHeap::do_collection(bool,bool,
unsigned,bool,int)+0x676
V   [libjvm.so+0x572743]   void
GenCollectedHeap::do_full_collection
(bool,int)+0x4f
V   [libjvm.so+0x217f6a]   void VM_GenCollectFull::doit()+0xa6
V   [libjvm.so+0x1d05df]   void VM_Operation::evaluate()+0x77
V   [libjvm.so+0x14aa82]   void VMThread::loop()+0x496
V   [libjvm.so+0x14a4d0]   void VMThread::run()+0x98
V   [libjvm.so+0x85a40d]   java_start+0xaf5
C   [libc.so.1+0xbd673]   _thrp_setup+0x9b
C   [libc.so.1+0xbd920]   _lwp_start+0x0
```

The crash happened in `objArrayKlass::oop_follow_contents(oopDesc*)` at program counter (pc) `0xfe20af22`. The preceding listing taken from the hs_err file shows the stack trace of the crash.

When the running process crashes, a core file gets generated. Let's debug this core file with HSDB and try to find the cause of this crash.

Launch HSDB to open the core file using the following command, and then, as shown in Figure 4.51, specify the location of the core file and location of the Java executable that was used to run the program:

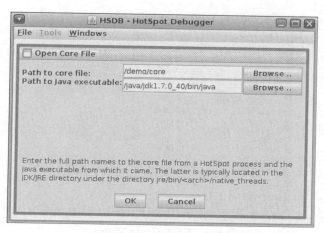

Figure 4.51 HSDB—Open Core File

```
oracle@solaris_11X $ export PATH=$JAVA_HOME/bin/:$PATH
oracle@solaris_11X $ java -classpath $JAVA_HOME/lib/sa-jdi.jar
sun.jvm.hotspot.HSDB
```

Figure 4.52 shows the disassembly of the code that was being executed around PC `0xfe20af22` when the crash happened.

The program counters and corresponding assembly instructions shown in Figure 4.52 indicate that the process crashed when trying to access the value at address `eax+100`, which is at program counter `0xfe20af22`. From the hs_err file, we can see the contents of the registers, and the value in the EAX register was:

```
EAX=0x2e617661, EBX=0xe7ab6e00, ECX=0x4a206f6c, EDX=0x00000004
ESP=0xe783ff90, EBP=0xe783ffc8, ESI=0xe7a4ea68, EDI=0x00000000
EIP=0xfe20af22, EFLAGS=0x00010297
```

To find out what was at `0x2e617661` and determine why the crash happened while attempting to read the value at `0x2e617661+100` we can use HSDB's Find Pointer panel, shown in Figure 4.53, to see that this address does not lie in the Java heap.

Figure 4.52 Code Viewer

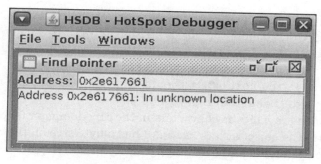

Figure 4.53 Find Pointer

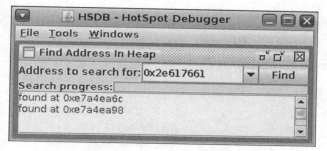

Figure 4.54 Find Address in Heap

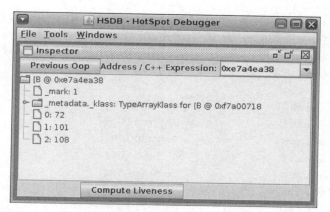

Figure 4.55 Oop Inspector showing object at `0xe7a4ea38`

Using the Find Address in Heap tool, we can find all the locations in the Java heap from where this particular address is referenced. See Figure 4.54.

Now, examine these found locations in the Object Inspector (see Figure 4.55) to see if the addresses lie within some valid objects.

All the found addresses bring up the byte array object at 0xe7a4ea38 in the Object Inspector, which means the object at 0xe7a4ea38 is the closest valid object just before these locations. If we look carefully, these locations actually go beyond the limits of the byte array object, which should have ended at 0xe7a4ea48, and from address 0xe7a4ea48 the next object should have started. See the raw contents at memory location 0xe7a4ea38 in Figure 4.56.

We can look at the raw bits as characters in the dbx debugger (shown below). This clearly shows that the object at 0xe7a4ea38 has a byte stream that goes beyond its size limit of three elements and overwrites the object starting at 0xe7a4ea48.

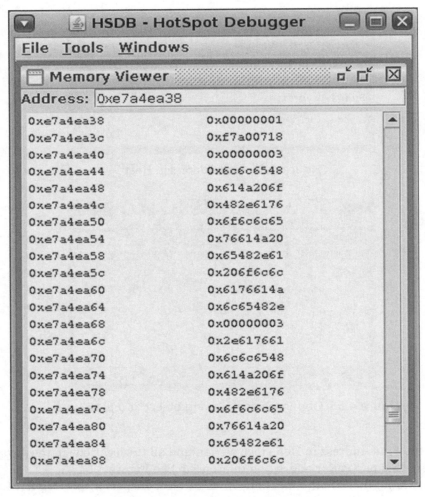

Figure 4.56 Memory Viewer

```
(dbx) x 0xe7a4ea38/100c
0xe7a4ea38:      '\001' '\0' '\0' '\0' '\030' '\007' '�' '�' '\003' '\0'
'\0' '\0' 'H' 'e' 'l' 'l'
0xe7a4ea48:      'o' ' ' 'J' 'a' 'v' 'a' '.' 'H' 'e' 'l' 'l' 'o' ' ' 'J'
'a' 'v'
0xe7a4ea58:      'a' '.' 'H' 'e' 'l' 'l' 'o' ' ' 'J' 'a' 'v' 'a' '.' 'H'
'e' 'l'
0xe7a4ea68:      '\003' '\0' '\0' '\0' 'a' 'v' 'a' '.' 'H' 'e' 'l' 'l' 'o'
' ' 'J' 'a'
0xe7a4ea78:      'v' 'a' '.' 'H' 'e' 'l' 'l' 'o' ' ' 'J' 'a' 'v' 'a' '.'
'H' 'e'
0xe7a4ea88:      'l' 'l' 'o' ' ' 'J' 'a' 'v' 'a' '.' 'H' 'e' 'l' 'l' 'o' ' '
'J'
0xe7a4ea98:      'a' 'v' 'a' '.'
```

This gives us a big clue. Now, we can easily search in the code where the bytes "Hello Java.Hello Java..." are being written and find the buggy part of the code that overflows a byte array. The following shows the faulty lines in our JNI code:

```
jclass cls = env->GetObjectClass(obj);
jfieldID fldID = env->GetFieldID(cls, "array", "[B");
jbyteArray arrayObject = (jbyteArray)env->GetObjectField(obj, fldID);
jbyte* array = (jbyte*)env->GetPrimitiveArrayCritical(arrayObject, 0);
memcpy(array, "Hello Java.Hello
Java.Hello Java.Hello Java.Hello
Java.Hello Java.Hello Java.Hello Java.Hello Java.", 100);
env->ReleasePrimitiveArrayCritical(arrayObject, array, 0);
```

The line memcpy(array, "Hello Java.Hello Java.Hello Java.Hello Java.Hello Java.Hello Java.Hello Java.Hello Java.", 100); is the culprit, which is writing to the byte array beyond its size limit.

Hmm . . . wasn't this fun? Debugging a crash with the SA tools!

Appendix

Additional HotSpot VM Command-Line Options of Interest

This appendix contains a listing of Java HotSpot VM (HotSpot VM) command-line options that may be of interest for the use or tuning of G1 GC. It also contains some command-line options that were not included or documented in the *Java™ Performance* appendix "HotSpot VM Command Line Options of Interest."

For each VM command-line option listed, there is a description of what the command-line options does, and also when it is appropriate to consider using it. The general recommendation for using HotSpot VM command-line options is to first have a justification for using the command-line option. You should resist the temptation to use a command-line option simply because it may have been used by someone else with some other application, or you read in a blog posting that someone used it. You should collect performance data while running your Java application when using the command-line option as the means for justifying the use of a command-line option.

HotSpot VM command-line options take one of two general forms. First, there are command-line options that are boolean in nature, that is, they are toggled on or off with a "+" or a "-" character ahead of the command-line option name, for example, -XX:+PrintAdaptiveSizePolicy, which uses a "+" character, toggles on, or enables, the command-line option called PrintAdaptiveSizePolicy. Likewise, the -XX:-PrintAdaptiveSizePolicy command-line option toggles off, or disables, the command-line option PrintAdaptiveSizePolicy.

The second form of HotSpot VM command-line options takes a numerical value, or a list of specific keywords. This appendix does not include any command-line options of the latter kind. The former kind that take a numerical value do not use the "+" or "-" character ahead of the command-line option name. For instance, -XX:ConcGCThreads is a command-line option that expects a numeric value such as -XX:ConcGCThreads=6.

The default values for a given HotSpot VM command-line option mentioned in this appendix are based on the option's default value in JDK 8u45. As a result, there may be some cases where a given command-line option has a different default value from what is mentioned in this appendix. Changes in default values usually occur due to additional information or input on the behavior of the command-line option at an alternative value.

-XX:+UseG1GC

Enables the G1 garbage collector. To use G1 in both Java 7 and Java 8 releases, it must be explicitly enabled using this command-line option. As of this writing, there are plans to make G1 the default GC for Java 9, though there is a possibility of reverting back to Parallel GC prior to Java 9's release.

-XX:ConcGCThreads

Sets the number of threads that the GC should use when doing work concurrently with the Java application. By default this is roughly one-fourth of the number of threads used to perform GC work when the Java threads are stopped.

Reducing -XX:ConcGCThreads can lead to higher throughput performance since fewer GC threads compete with the Java application for CPU usage. Too few concurrent threads may cause the concurrent cycle to not complete fast enough to reclaim memory.

-XX:G1HeapRegionSize

Sets the size of the heap regions for G1. By default this is about 1/2000 of the heap size. Possible region sizes are 1M, 2M, 4M, 8M, 16M, and 32M.

Objects that are larger than half the region size need to be managed specially by G1. Increasing the region size allows larger objects to be allocated with the normal allocation path, which may help performance if such large objects are common. However, having larger regions means that G1 has less flexibility when it comes to making ergonomic decisions, such as, for example, deciding on the size of the young generation.

-XX:G1HeapWastePercent

Controls the acceptable amount of free memory that G1 will not collect. By default this value is 5 percent.

G1 will collect all regions until any regions left would only free up -XX:G1HeapWastePercent of memory. Especially on large heaps it can make sense to use a lower value for -XX:G1HeapWastePercent, since 5 percent of the heap size represents a fairly large amount of memory.

-XX:G1MixedGCCountTarget

Sets the target value for how many mixed GCs should be performed after a concurrent cycle. The default value is 8.

Old regions normally take a little longer to collect than young regions. Allowing more mixed GCs after a concurrent cycle allows G1 to spread out the reclamation of the old regions over more collections. But increasing -XX:G1MixedGCCountTarget also means that it will take longer until a new concurrent cycle can be started. If mixed GC pause times are too long, it may help to increase -XX:G1MixedGCCountTarget.

-XX:+G1PrintRegionLivenessInfo

This is a diagnostic VM option, and as such it needs to be enabled with -XX:+Unlock DiagnosticVMOptions. When enabled, it will print liveness information for each region on the heap. The information includes the usage, the size of the remembered set, and the "GC efficiency," which is a measure of how valuable it is to collect this region. The information is logged after a marking cycle has completed and also after the regions have been sorted for inclusion in the collection set.

The information logged by -XX:+G1PrintRegionLivenessInfo can be useful when trying to understand the heap usage and to identify issues with remembered sets. Since it logs one line for each region in the heap, the data can be hard to manage for large heaps.

-XX:G1ReservePercent

To reduce the risk of getting a promotion failure, G1 reserves some memory for promotions. This memory will not be used for the young generation. By default G1 keeps 10 percent of the heap reserved for this purpose.

On a large heap with a large live set, 10 percent of the heap may be too much to reserve. Reducing this value can leave more memory for the young generation and lead to longer times between GCs, which normally increases throughput performance.

-XX:+G1SummarizeRSetStats

This is a diagnostic VM option, and as such it needs to be enabled with -XX:+UnlockDiagnosticVMOptions. When enabled, it will print a detailed summary about the remembered sets when the VM exits. In combination with -XX:G1SummarizeRSetStatsPeriod this summary can be printed periodically instead of just at VM exit.

If remembered set issues are suspected, this can be a useful tool to analyze them.

-XX:G1SummarizeRSetStatsPeriod

This is a diagnostic VM option, and as such it needs to be enabled with -XX:+UnlockDiagnosticVMOptions. It can only be used together with -XX:+G1SummarizeRSetStats. If set to a value other than 0, this will print the same summary produced by -XX:+G1SummarizeRSetStats. But instead of printing it just on VM exit, it will print it each time after the number of GCs specified as the -XX:G1SummarizeRSetStatsPeriod has occurred.

It can be expensive to print this information for every GC, but printing it periodically makes it possible to identify trends in the remembered set management.

-XX:+G1TraceConcRefinement

This is a diagnostic VM option, and as such it needs to be enabled in combination with -XX:+UnlockDiagnosticVMOptions. With -XX:+G1TraceConcRefinement enabled, information about the concurrent refinement threads is logged.

The information produced includes when concurrent refinement threads are activated and when they are deactivated. This can be useful to identify issues with concurrent refinement.

-XX:+G1UseAdaptiveConcRefinement

When enabled, this command-line option dynamically recalculates the values for -XX:G1ConcRefinementGreenZone, -XX:G1ConcRefinementYellowZone, and -XX:G1ConcRefinementRedZone every GC. This flag is enabled by default.

-XX:GCTimeRatio

Sets the time spent in the Java application threads compared to that spent in the GC threads.

G1 attempts to honor the value set for -XX:GCTimeRatio to ensure that the Java application threads get enough execution time as specified by this command-line option. G1 does this by splitting work up and aborting work that can be split up or aborted. G1 also tries to spread out GC pauses to accomplish this goal. The default value for -XX:GCTimeRatio can vary depending on the garbage collector in use by the HotSpot VM. When G1 is in use, the default -XX:GCTimeRatio is 9.

The HotSpot VM converts the -XX:GCTimeRatio value to a percentage using the following formula: 100/(1 + GCTimeRatio). In other words, -XX:GCTimeRatio can be thought of as asking the HotSpot VM to attempt to spend no more than 100/(1 + GCTimeRatio) percent of its time executing in the GC threads. Hence, a default value of -XX:GCTimeRatio=9 with G1 means that up to 10 percent of the time can be spent doing GC work.

It should be noted that the HotSpot VM's throughput garbage collector, Parallel GC, sets a default value for -XX:GCTimeRatio=99. This means that the HotSpot VM should attempt to spend up to 1 percent of its time doing GC work. This makes sense since Parallel GC is the throughput GC in contrast to G1, which is intended to be a more balanced throughput, latency, and memory footprint type of GC.

-XX:+HeapDumpBeforeFullGC

When this command-line option is enabled, an hprof file is created just prior to a full GC starting. The hprof file is created in the directory where the HotSpot VM is launched.

Comparing the contents of the Java heap before and after a full GC using this command-line option in conjunction with -XX:+HeapDumpAfterFullGC can give a good indication of memory leaks and other issues.

-XX:+HeapDumpAfterFullGC

When this command-line option is enabled, an hprof file is created right after the full GC has completed. The hprof file is created in the directory where the HotSpot VM is launched.

Comparing the contents of the Java heap before and after a full GC using this command-line option in conjunction with -XX:+HeapDumpBeforeFullGC can give a good indication of memory leaks and other issues.

-XX:InitiatingHeapOccupancyPercent

Sets the value for when a concurrent cycle in G1 should be started. The default value is 45. In other words, after a GC, G1 measures the occupancy of the old generation space and compares that to the current Java heap size. If the occupancy of the old generation space reaches or exceeds the InitiatingHeapOccupancyPercent, then a G1 concurrent cycle is initiated by scheduling an initial-mark operation to begin on the next GC. The G1 concurrent cycle is the means by which G1 concurrently collects the old generation space. A concurrent cycle begins with an initial-mark operation, which can be observed in the GC logs with the -XX:+PrintGC Details command-line option.

If full GCs are occurring due to the old generation running out of available space, lowering this value will initiate a concurrent cycle earlier to avoid exhausting available space.

If no full GCs are occurring and it is desirable to increase throughput, it may help to increase this value to get fewer concurrent cycles. G1 concurrent cycles do require CPU cycles to execute and therefore may steal CPU cycles from application threads. Hence, frequent G1 concurrent cycles can reduce peak throughput. However, it is generally better to err with G1 concurrent cycles running too early rather than too late. If G1 concurrent cycles are run too late, the consequence is likely to be frequent full GCs, which of course introduces undesirable lengthy GC pauses.

See also -XX:+G1UseAdaptiveIHOP.

-XX:+UseStringDeduplication

Enables the deduplication of Java Strings. This command-line option and feature was introduced in JDK 8u20. String deduplication is disabled by default.

When enabled, this option deduplicates `String`s by looking at the `String`'s underlying character array. When a `String` contains a sequence of characters equal to another `String`'s sequence of characters, such as if `string1.equals(string2)` evaluates to `true`, the `String` objects are updated to share the same underlying `String` character array. The end result is the freeing of space required by the duplicate character array having the same sequence of characters. It should be noted that the `String` objects are actually not deduplicated; rather their underlying character arrays are deduplicated.

This feature is implemented only with the G1 garbage collector. While enabling this command-line option is allowed with the other non-G1 HotSpot collectors— Parallel GC, CMS GC, and Serial GC—no `String` deduplication is performed when enabled.

An object is considered a deduplication candidate if all of the following statements are true:

- The object is an instance of `java.lang.String`.
- The object is being evacuated from a young heap region.
- The object is being evacuated to a young/survivor heap region and the object's age is equal to the deduplication age threshold, or the object is being evacuated to an old heap region and the object's age is less than the deduplication age threshold. See `-XX:StringDeduplicationAgeThreshold` for additional information on the deduplication threshold.

Interned `String`s are dealt with differently from noninterned `String`s. Interned `String`s are explicitly deduplicated just before being inserted into the internal HotSpot VM's `StringTable` to avoid counteracting HotSpot Server JIT compiler optimizations done on `String` literals.

See also `-XX:StringDeduplicationAgeThreshold` and `-XX:+PrintString DeduplicationStatistics`.

-XX:StringDeduplicationAgeThreshold

Sets the `String` object age threshold when a `String` object is considered a candidate for deduplication. The default value is 3.

More specifically, a `String` becomes a candidate for deduplication once a `String` object has been promoted to a G1 old region, or its age is higher than the deduplication age threshold. Once a `String` has become a candidate for deduplication, or has been deduplicated, it will never become a candidate again. This approach avoids making the same object a candidate more than once.

Also see `-XX:+UseStringDeduplication` and `-XX:+PrintString DeduplicationStatistics`.

-XX:+PrintStringDeduplicationStatistics

Enables the printing of `String` deduplication statistics. The default value is disabled.

This command-line option can be very helpful when you want to know if enabling deduplication will result in a significant savings in the amount of space in use by `String` objects in the Java heap. Hence, enabling this command-line option provides data that justifies whether there may be value in enabling -XX:+UseStringDeduplication.

Also see -XX:+UseStringDeduplication and -XX:StringDeduplicationAgeThreshold.

-XX:+G1UseAdaptiveIHOP

This is a new command-line option available in JDK 9 and later. It adaptively adjusts the initiating heap occupancy threshold from the initial value of the command-line option `InitiatingHeapOccupancyPercent`. The intent is to let G1 adapt the marking threshold to application behavior so as to increase throughput by triggering the marking cycle as late as possible yet not exhaust old generation space.

The mechanism enabled by `G1UseAdaptiveIHOP` uses the value of the command-line option `InitiatingHeapOccupancyPercent` as an initial value for the marking cycles until sufficient observations about the application behavior have been made. It then adaptively adjusts to a more optimal heap occupancy percent at which to start the marking cycle.

When `G1UseAdaptiveIHOP` is disabled (when -XX:-G1UseAdaptiveIHOP is explicitly specified as a command-line option), G1 will always use the `InitiatingHeap OccupancyPercent` value as the occupancy at which to start the marking cycle.

`G1UseAdaptiveIHOP`, as of this writing, will be enabled by default with its introduction in JDK 9.

See also -XX:InitiatingHeapOccupancyPercent.

-XX:MaxGCPauseMillis

This command-line option sets the pause time goal in milliseconds for G1. The default value is 200. Note that this is a goal, not a hard maximum pause time that G1 can never exceed.

G1 attempts to size the young generation to make sure that it can be collected within the goal set by -XX:MaxGCPauseMillis. When G1 is in use, this command-line option, along with sizing the Java heap with -Xms and –Xmx, is the command-line option that is expected to be used. These three command-line options are also the suggested starting point when using G1, even when migrating from Parallel GC or CMS GC to G1.

-XX:MinHeapFreeRatio

Sets the value for how much memory is allowed to be free on the heap. The default value is 40. The value is actually a percentage, not a ratio. It is unfortunate that the command-line name includes the term *ratio*.

The Java HotSpot VM uses the value set by -XX:MinHeapFreeRatio to help determine when to grow the Java heap. This decision is made during a GC and can be described thus: if less than -XX:MinHeapFreeRatio percent of the Java heap is free, G1 will attempt to grow the Java heap to meet the value set as the -XX:MinHeapFreeRatio.

Obviously, in order for the Java heap size to grow, the values set for -Xms, the initial Java heap size, and -Xmx, the maximum Java heap size, must be set to different values. If -Xms and -Xmx are set to the same value, the Java HotSpot VM will not grow or shrink the Java heap.

-XX:MaxHeapFreeRatio

Sets the value for how little memory is allowed to be free on the heap. The default value is 70. Similarly to -XX:MinHeapFreeRatio, the value is actually a percentage, not a ratio. Again, similarly to -XX:MinHeapFreeRatio, it is unfortunate that the command-line name includes the term *ratio*.

The Java HotSpot VM uses the value set by -XX:MaxHeapFreeRatio to help determine when to shrink the Java heap. This decision is made during a GC and can be described thus: if more than -XX:MaxHeapFreeRatio percent of the Java heap is free, G1 will attempt to shrink the Java heap to meet the value set as the -XX:MaxHeapFreeRatio.

Also as is the case with -XX:MinHeapFreeRatio, in order for the Java heap size to shrink, the values set for -Xms, the initial Java heap size, and -Xmx, the maximum Java heap size, must be set to different values. If -Xms and -Xmx are set to the same value, the Java HotSpot VM will not shrink or grow the Java heap.

-XX:+PrintAdaptiveSizePolicy

Turns on logging of information about heap size changes. This information can be very useful in understanding the ergonomic heuristic decisions made by G1 (also applicable to Parallel GC).

Use of -XX:+PrintAdaptiveSizePolicy in tuning G1 is described in Chapter 3, "Garbage First Garbage Collector Performance Tuning."

-XX:+ResizePLAB

Sets whether the thread-local allocation buffers that the GC uses for promoting objects should be resized dynamically or just have a static size. The default value is true.

The dynamic resizing of the PLABs in G1 has been shown to cause some performance issues. For some applications, disabling the resizing of thread-local promotion buffers can improve performance by reducing the duration the G1 GC pauses.

-XX:+ResizeTLAB

Sets whether the thread-local allocation buffers that the Java application threads use for Java object allocations should be resized dynamically or have a static fixed size. The default is `true`.

In most cases the TLAB resizing improves application performance by reducing contention in the allocation path. Contrary to the PLAB sizing, it is not very common to see that turning this off is good for performance. Hence, for almost all applications, it is best to leave this command-line option enabled, which again is its default.

-XX:+ClassUnloadingWithConcurrentMark

Turns on class unloading during G1 concurrent cycles, the concurrent collection of old generation. The default is `true`.

Normally it is beneficial to be able to unload unreachable classes during G1 concurrent cycles rather than having to rely on full GCs to do so. The unloading of classes during G1 concurrent cycles can sometimes increase G1 remark GC times. If G1 remark pause times are higher than can be tolerated to meet GC pause time goals, and few classes are expected to be unreachable, it may be beneficial to disable this option, that is, `-XX:-ClassUnloadingWithConcurrentMark`.

-XX:+ClassUnloading

Turns class unloading on and off. The default value is `true`, meaning the HotSpot VM will unload unreachable classes. If this command-line option is disabled—that is, `-XX:-ClassUnloading`—the HotSpot VM will not unload any unreachable classes, ever, not even as part of full GCs.

-XX:+UnlockDiagnosticVMOptions

Sets whether flags tagged as diagnostic options should be allowed or not. The default is `false`.

There are some command-line options that are tagged as "diagnostic." These can be seen in a list of Java HotSpot VM command-line options using the `-XX:+PrintFlags Final` in conjunction with `-XX:+UnlockDiagnosticVMOptions`. "Diagnostic" options have a field {*diagnostic*} command-line option type listed in the `-XX:+PrintFlags Final` output. Examples of diagnostic HotSpot VM command-line options include `-XX:+G1PrintRegionLivenessInfo`, which prints detailed liveness information for each G1 region on each GC, and `-XX:+LogCompilation`, which produces information about optimization decisions the Java HotSpot VM's JIT compiler has made.

Diagnostic options tend to introduce additional overhead to normal execution and are generally used to investigate or diagnose unexpected behavior of the Java HotSpot VM or the application it is executing.

-XX:+UnlockExperimentalVMOptions

Sets whether flags tagged as experimental options should be allowed or not. The default is false.

Similar to -XX:+UnlockDiagnosticVMOptions, there are some command-line options that are tagged as "experimental." These can be seen in a list of Java HotSpot VM command-line options using the -XX:+PrintFlagsFinal in conjunction with -XX:+UnlockExperimentalVMOptions. "Experimental" options have a field {experimental} command-line option type listed in the -XX:+PrintFlagsFinal output.

It is important to note experimental command-line options are not part of the officially supported Java SE product—but are available for experimenting with—yet offer additional capabilities that may be worth exploring for some user cases.

Some experimental command-line options may be performance related features but may not have undergone full scrutiny or rigorous quality assurance testing. Yet, they may offer performance benefits in some use cases.

An example of an experimental command-line option is -XX:G1NewSizePercent, which controls the minimum size of G1 can reduce the young generation relative to the Java heap size. It defaults to 5. In other words, the minimum size G1 can adaptively size young generation is 5% of the Java heap size. For some use cases where very low GC pause times are desired, one could experiment in a non-production environment setting a lower -XX:G1NewSizePercent to say 1 or 2, yet realizing in doing so there is no official product support.

To use an experimental option, the -XX:+UnlockExperimentalVMOptions must be specified in conjunction with the experimental command-line option. For example, to use the -XX:G1NewSizePercent=2 command-line option, you would specify both -XX:+UnlockExperimentalVMOptions -XX:G1NewSizePercent=2. The -XX:+UnlockExperimentalVMOptions only need be specified once if more than one experimental command-line option is desired.

-XX:+UnlockCommercialFeatures

Sets whether Oracle-specific features that require a license are to be enabled. The default is false.

There are some capabilities or features developed by Oracle that are available only via the Oracle Java runtime distributed by Oracle and are not included in OpenJDK. An example of an Oracle commercial feature is Java Flight Recorder, which is part of Oracle's monitoring and management tool called Java Mission Control. Java Flight Recorder is a profiling and event collection framework that can collect and show within Java Mission Control low-level information about how the application and JVM are behaving.

Index

REGISTER YOUR PRODUCT at informit.com/register
Access Additional Benefits and SAVE 35% on Your Next Purchase

- Download available product updates.
- Access bonus material when applicable.
- Receive exclusive offers on new editions and related products.
  (Just check the box to hear from us when setting up your account.)
- Get a coupon for 35% for your next purchase, valid for 30 days. Your code will be available in your InformIT cart. (You will also find it in the Manage Codes section of your account page.)

Registration benefits vary by product. Benefits will be listed on your account page under Registered Products.

InformIT.com—The Trusted Technology Learning Source
InformIT is the online home of information technology brands at Pearson, the world's foremost education company. At InformIT.com you can

- Shop our books, eBooks, software, and video training.
- Take advantage of our special offers and promotions (informit.com/promotions).
- Sign up for special offers and content newsletters (informit.com/newsletters).
- Read free articles and blogs by information technology experts.
- Access thousands of free chapters and video lessons.

Connect with InformIT—Visit informit.com/community
Learn about InformIT community events and programs.

informIT.com
the trusted technology learning source

Addison-Wesley • Cisco Press • IBM Press • Microsoft Press • Pearson IT Certification • Prentice Hall • Que • Sams • VMware Press

ALWAYS LEARNING   PEARSON